AF478183

Public Sociology and Civil Society

Public Sociology and Civil Society

Governance, Politics, and Power

Patricia Mooney Nickel

Paradigm Publishers
Boulder • London

Copyright © 2012 Paradigm Publishers

Published in the United States by Paradigm Publishers, 2845 Wilderness Place, Boulder, CO 80301 USA.

Paradigm Publishers is the trade name of Birkenkamp & Company, LLC, Dean Birkenkamp, President and Publisher.

Library of Congress Cataloging-in-Publication Data
Nickel, Patricia Mooney.
  Public sociology and civil society : governance, politics, and power / Patricia Mooney Nickel.
       p. cm.
  Includes bibliographical references and index.
  ISBN 978-1-59451-976-5 (hardback : alk. paper)
  1. Sociology—Philosophy. 2. Applied sociology. 3. Sociology—Methodology.
4. Civil society. I. Title.
  HM511.N53 2012
  301.01—dc23

                                                                 2011030057

Printed and bound in the United States of America on acid-free paper that meets the standards of the American National Standard for Permanence of Paper for Printed Library Materials.

Designed and Typeset by Straight Creek Bookmakers.

16 15 14 13 12   1 2 3 4 5

Contents

Part III: Power and Practice

Acknowledgments

I would like to express my gratitude to Ben Agger, Chamsy el-Oljeili, Timothy W. Luke, and Barry Smart for their generous and engaged dialogue as this project evolved. Thanks to Angela M. Eikenberry for her support of my critical views on governance and with whom I have a long-standing dialogue about civil society. I am grateful to the students in my honors seminars held at Victoria University of Wellington 2008–2010 for their humor and unique perspective on the topic. Perhaps more importantly, they demonstrated to me that students of public sociology, civil society, and governance are not only perfectly capable of understanding these topics through the lens of critical theory; they want to do so and often do so better than the authors with whom these concepts originate! My research assistant, Florence Fudakowska, did an excellent job of navigating the ins and outs of bibliographic presentation. Thanks to Ed Nickel for all of the little things that make a huge difference. Dennis Smith was the first editor to give my ideas about public sociology a thorough review, and I am very grateful to him for this. Finally, I want to thank Dean Birkenkamp for his patience and for supporting an interdisciplinary project.

Chapter 1

Introduction

Public Sociology and Civil Society in the Context of Governance

This is a book about public sociology only by way of an access point; through the lens of public sociology, it is a book about the contemporary practices of governing. Public sociology responds to significantly more than sociology's relationship with the public. Over the past ten years the phrase *public sociology* has been used to refer to efforts to build civil society (Burawoy 2005a), the management of nongovernmental organizations (NGOs) (American University 2007, 2010), program evaluation (Humboldt State University 2010), cosmopolitan state management (Beck 2005b; Delanty 2006), social gerontology (Putney, et al. 2007), and government policy consultancy (Perrucci, et al. 2008). Whether they involve the governing vocabulary of democratic ideals or the practice of knowledge, the circulation of these multiple meanings is a technique of governing.

In considering public sociology, civil society, and governance together, I want to understand the "kinship between the lines of inquiry and the proximity of those who undertook them" (Foucault 1998, 439). My aim is therefore to explore the politics of academic disciplines, knowledge, and discourse as they have emerged within the recent debate over public sociology, while also highlighting how this debate has become intertwined with civil society and what has been hailed as an age of "radically democratic governance" (Sørensen and Torfing 2005a). What does it mean to practice knowledge publically and to govern democratically? How are these two activities—the production of knowledge and governing—related?

I understand *public sociology, civil society,* and *governance* to be interrelated terms that have as much potential to become sites of disciplinary discourse as they do to become sites of radical politics. In advancing this argument I assume that knowledge and its organization are political. Knowledge production by intellectuals is political in the sense that it can be viewed as a powerful means of either stabilizing or challenging the patterns according to which people live their lives, be they patterns of ideas, expectations, governments, economies, or so-called laws of society. The organization of knowledge is political in the sense that it is situated within universities, which are not distinct from the state or the economy and associated demands for the production of instrumental knowledge (Apple 1993, 2003; Aronowitz 2000; Barrow 1990; Luke 2005). This is to say, first, that the pursuit and organization of knowledge involve deliberate choices made by individuals with preferences about how the world should be understood, and, second, that these choices are significantly influenced by the requirements of governing and the knowledge economy within which intellectuals are situated.

The Impetus: Contemporary Calls for Public Sociology

A central impetus for this inquiry is my observation of the recent widespread and often intersecting circulation of phrases like *public sociology, civil society,* and *democratic governance* within varying academic disciplines, as well as within the varying institutions of practice where public service now takes place. The contemporary call for public sociology, because it explicitly references civil society and governance, provides a starting point for untangling these concepts.

Public sociology in its early conception described a style of intellectuality involving dialogue between sociologists and the publics with whom they were concerned. Beyond this broad framing, what type of dialogue, with what purpose, which publics, and the functions of intellectuals and the knowledge they produce in relationship to civil society and the state are now widely contested. The label *public sociologist* as a descriptor of public intellectuals within the discipline of sociology originates as early as Herbert J. Gans's 1988 Presidential Address to the American Sociological Association (ASA), titled "Sociology in America: The Discipline and the Public." Drawing on Russell Jacoby's (2000) notion of the public intellectual, Gans (1989) specifies that public sociologists are *not* popularizers of sociology, but rather "they are empirical researchers, analysts, or theorists like the rest of us, although often their work is particularly thoughtful, imaginative, or original in some respect" (7). For Gans, public sociologists share three traits. First, they enjoy the craft of writing and are therefore particularly adept at conveying complex ideas. Second, they have broad sociological interests; they understand the world outside of narrow disciplinary boundaries. Third, they avoid "undue professionalism" (Gans 1989, 7). Echoing Gans's concern about the impact of the professionalization of knowledge on public life, in his 2000 Presidential Address to the ASA, titled "Social Justice for Sociology: Agendas for the Twenty-First Century," Joe Feagin (2001) argued for a sociology that addressed major public problems: "creating and ensuring the processes of a truly democratic participation in decision-making" (5).

Contemporary statements of the need for public sociology echo the tone used by Robert S. Lynd (1967), writing about the urgent need for the social sciences to address social problems in the wake of the Great Depression: "a prevalent mood among sophisticated persons today is a sense of hopelessness in the face of the too-bigness of the issues we confront ... we are today attempting to live in the most disparate and confusing cultural environment faced by any generation of Americans since the beginning of our national life" (11). Twenty years and a world war later, in 1959, C. Wright Mills (2000) observed among people a feeling "that their private lives are a series of traps. They sense that within their everyday worlds, they cannot overcome their troubles ..." (3). The same could be said of individuals today. Lynd and Mills were writing in the wake of an industrial revolution accompanied by urbanization and an associated rise in bureaucracy, two world wars and an associated instrumentalization of knowledge as a means to govern through technological advance, and a transformation to mass consumerism. Intellectuals today write in the wake of another technological revolution (information), another transformation of space (Internet, globalization), another bureaucratic transformation in a shift from government to governance, and another transformation of consumerism (e.g., green consumerism, philanthrocapitalism). These rapid changes and the sense of what Mills called "private troubles" being divorced from "public problems" inspired Mills to write famously of the "sociological imagination," which often is discussed in calls for public sociology. "The sociological imagination enables us to grasp history and biography and the relations between the two in society" (Mills 2000, 6). This involves understanding how one's private troubles are part of bigger public problems—public problems that we realize, *in contrast to professional and disciplinary knowledge,* that we have the ability to publicly debate and change in order to improve our lives.

Over the past ten years there have been two substantial appeals for a renewed emphasis on public sociology. The first is Ben Agger's (2000) *Public Sociology: From Social Facts to Literary Acts,* now in its second (2007) edition. For Agger (2007), like Mills, Gans, and Feagin, public sociology is a mode of writing that reveals that it is a subjective authoring rather than an objective observation, engages in self-translation with a public in mind, and addresses major public issues.

> A sociology is public if it embraces Marx's eleventh thesis on Feuerbach, which merges theory and practice, and if it recognizes that method doesn't solve all intellectual problems but is merely one form of rhetoric (discourse) among many. A public sociology must want to change the world, and it must recognize that it is already changing the world by intervening in it. Finally, a public sociology addresses itself to various publics, to which it doesn't condescend but that it seeks to mobilize. (270)

Agger's emphasis here is not on preserving the discipline of sociology, per se, but on the transformation of sociological discourse.

In many ways, Agger's call for public sociology is an extension of his earlier work on the sociology of public life, including *The Decline of Discourse* (1990) and *A Critical Theory of Public Life* (1991b). The key point to take from Agger is that, although public intellectuality is important, public discourse depends on more than intellectuals speaking authoritatively in public; the conditions for public discourse must be cultivated through public writing that challenges the value-neutrality of knowledge, which is to say that it recognizes that it is one portrayal among many. This mode of intellectuality requires that sociologists reveal in dialogue with the public that the production of knowledge involves individual passions about its reception; we cannot help but infuse the knowledge that we produce with our own purpose. For example, I am a critical intellectual, and this significantly influences my framing of public sociology; although I attempt to present a wide spectrum of ideas, I cannot help but make deliberate choices about what matters when we think about public sociology. Although my account might be empirically accurate, it remains the outcome of my value-laden choice of what to portray as important. Revealing this fact leaves open a space for my readers to contest my framing and thus instigates dialogue.

The second, and perhaps best known, recent conceptualization of public sociology was first articulated by Michael Burawoy at Boston College in 2004 and further elaborated in his 2004 Presidential Address to the ASA, titled "For Public Sociology." Burawoy (2007a) defines public sociology as "a sociology that seeks to bring sociology to publics beyond the academy, promoting dialogue about issues that affect the fate of society, placing the values to which we adhere under a microscope" (104). This definition is constructed through his (2005a, 11) portrayal of sociology as a division of labor, which is shown in Table 1-1.

The functions of the sociological laborers in Table 1-1 are portrayed by Burawoy (2005a) as:

Table 1-1 Burawoy's Division of Labor

	Academic Audience	*Extra-Academic Audience*
Instrumental Knowledge	PROFESSIONAL	POLICY
Reflexive Knowledge	CRITICAL	PUBLIC

- **Professional/Instrumental/Academic:** "Research conducted within research programs that define assumptions, theories, concepts, questions, and puzzles" (12).
- **Policy/Instrumental/Extra-Academic:** "Defense of sociological research, human subjects, funding, congressional briefings" (12).
- **Critical/Reflexive/Academic:** "Critical debates of the discipline within and between research programs" (12).
- **Public/Reflexive/Extra-Academic:** "Concern for the public image of sociology, presenting findings in an accessible manner, teaching basics of sociology and writing textbooks" (12).

In addition to four functional categories of labor, Burawoy identifies two types of knowledge and two types of audience, which break down as follows:

- **Instrumental/Professional/Academic**: theoretical/empirical knowledge, correspondent truth, legitimacy by scientific norms, accountability to peers
- **Instrumental/Policy/Extra-Academic**: concrete knowledge, pragmatic truth, legitimacy by effectiveness, accountability to clients
- **Reflexive/Critical/Academic**: foundational knowledge, normative truth, legitimacy by moral vision, accountability to critical intellectuals
- **Reflexive/Public/Extra-Academic**: communicative knowledge, consensus for truth, legitimacy by relevance, accountability to designated publics (16)

I will argue in Chapter Three that, through this organization of knowledge, Burawoy excludes from discourse a "nonprofessional" or "nonpublic" audience that *ought to be equally involved in criticizing the impact of professional sociology on their lives.* Unlike Agger, who emphasizes the sociology of discourse over the discipline of sociology, Burawoy is focused on stabilizing and popularizing professional sociology. Whereas Gans (1989) was careful to distinguish the public sociologist from the "visible scientist," who is a popularizer (7), for Burawoy (2005a) public sociologists have "concern for the public image of sociology, presenting findings in an accessible manner, teaching basics of sociology and writing textbooks" (12).

Burawoy's 2004 Presidential Address and the renewed ideal of public sociology has inspired many professional journal symposia, conference proceedings, newsletters, and curriculum developments over the past ten years and instigated a valuable debate about public sociology, as well as a wide range of social problems, including the academic career of the sociologist. Some of these debates are constructively critical and have included Burawoy in dialogue with other advocates of public sociology. Others have rejected the ideal of public sociology altogether and have attempted to "defend" sociology against politics, even publishing a Web site titled "Save Sociology," which "was developed in response to the various forms of attack on sociology as an academic discipline that have taken place in recent years, especially since the advent of so-called 'public' sociology. This [is] an attempt to safeguard the academic status and integrity of sociology" (Deflem 2010). (For a response see McLaughlin, et al. 2007.) Burawoy (2009a) characterizes this debate as "The Public Sociology Wars," which is telling of the impact of the suggestion that there is a legitimate intellectuality to be found *outside* the heavily guarded boundaries of fixed intellectual and disciplinary authority.

Intellectual authority and the legitimacy of knowledge are important considerations beyond the public sociology debate; they will also inform my consideration of the ideals of civil society and governance. From Agger's (1989a, 1989b, 1989c, 1990, 1991b, 2000) perspective, claims to objective intellectual authority potentially *inhibit* public discourse to the extent that the public fails to realize that the ideas produced by intellectuals are contestable. For Agger, the realization that knowledge is contestable is the foundation of public discourse. From Burawoy's (2005a) perspective, disciplinary/professional sociology is *foundational* to public sociology: "there can be neither policy nor public sociology without a *professional sociology* that supplies true and tested methods, accumulated bodies of knowledge, orienting questions, and conceptual frameworks" (10). In contrast, for Agger (1989b, 1990), professional sociology and its expert discourse *results* in a decline in discourse about public issues; the public patterns its everyday life after expert discourse rather than debating the contestable issues raised by public intellectuals who respect the public's own lifeworld-grounded knowledge of the world (Agger 1992a). In response to Burawoy's division of labor, Feagin, et al. (2009) were, like Agger, critical of the idea that public sociology will emerge from Burawoy's division of labor, arguing that professional sociology creates a discourse that is often "anti-public" (79).

As I will demonstrate in Chapters Two and Three, these two opposing views on the public impact of professional sociology and instrumental knowledge—for Agger professional sociology and instrumental knowledge result in a *decline* in public discourse; for Burawoy it is essential to the *legitimacy* of public sociology—point to the very possibility of a public that is receptive to public sociology, as well as to the possibility of a robust civil society and radically democratic governance. For Burawoy, the relationship between knowledge and public life is dependent on professional sociology and its associated norms of knowledge production. For Agger (1990), the relationship between knowledge and public life depends on the transformation of professional sociology, which is embedded in what he calls literary political economy: "We cannot comprehend, and thus remedy, the decline of discourse without considering the dominance of the university over intellectual life. *I am pointing to an absence* [of the public] *that is effectively a product of particular social and economic arrangements of knowledge*" (33–34).

The contemporary call for public sociology is therefore not as simple as it might first seem; there is widespread debate within sociology about the politics of knowledge. This has involved opposition to the suggestion that there is something political involved in doing sociology, as well as debate among advocates of public sociology in the tradition of Mills, Gans, Feagin, and Agger, who take issue with how Burawoy has framed the discipline and his division of labor. This is further complicated by the fact that the debates over public sociology involve words, concepts, institutions, and problems that transcend the disciplinary boundaries of sociology.

In particular, the word *public* now seems ubiquitous as a disciplinary modifier in the social sciences. As Jurgen Habermas (1991) observed in the opening of his seminal text, *The Structural Transformation of the Public Sphere: An Inquiry into a Category of Bourgeois Society,* the "usage of the words 'public' and 'public sphere' betrays a multiplicity of concurrent meanings" (1). The adjective *public* is problematic because it simultaneously refers to legal sectors (public and private), spheres of discourse and action (public sphere and private sphere), territories (public property and private property), and, as a disciplinary modifier, intellectuality (public and professional). These public-private-professional distinctions are further complicated by the fact that the boundaries themselves are porous: Private companies make donations to public entities, discourse and action in the public sphere influences private lives, private property is publicly subsidized, professional discourse has public impact, and public discourse has an impact on the profession.

At present there are at least ten academic foci modified by the adjective *public.* In addition to the traditional "applied fields" of public administration, public policy (which might also be policy sociology), public finance, and public law, the recent public turn in the social sciences includes calls for public anthropology (Borofsky 2000; Purcell 2000), public criminology (Chancer and McLaughlin 2007; Currie 2007), public geography (Murphy, et al. 2005; Murphy 2006), and public intellectual political scientists (Hauck 2010). Once preoccupied with establishing a legitimate claim to *scientific* knowledge, as David Paul Haney (2008) demonstrates in his study *The Americanization of Social Science,* the social sciences are now preoccupied not only with their scientific legitimacy, but also with their *public* scientific legitimacy as their surveys compete with brain scans over no less than "public neuroscience," "neuroeconomics," and the emerging field of "brain policy" (Blank 1999). It is no longer enough for the social sciences to be rigorous; now they must be rigorously popular at congressional hearings, on CNN, and in front of grant-making bodies that reinforce with grant dollars the legitimacy of their research questions, which were developed in the pursuit of grant dollars.

Whether because of mounting budgetary constraints and competition over grant funding or general insecurity at a time when so many "sciences" seem to be resulting in so many disasters, more and more academic disciplines are placing emphasis on their legitimate publicness, while also highlighting their contribution of "job skills" for the new economy. "Derek Bok, a former president of Harvard and the author of several books on higher education, argues, 'The humanities has a lot to contribute to the preparation of students for their vocational lives'" (Cohen 2009, C1). This is an unsurprising statement when *The New York Times* reported in 2009 that "in tough times, the humanities must justify their worth.... 'Although people in humanities have always lamented the state of the field, they have never felt quite as much of a panic that their field is becoming irrelevant,' said Andrew Delbanco, the director of American studies at Columbia University" (Cohen 2009, C1).

The subjection of the liberal arts, as well as the social sciences, to vocational concerns is not a new problem, but its labeling as public sociology, civil society, and governance is. In 1943 twelve men convened as The Committee on the Objectives of a General Education in a Free Society and subsequently published *General Education in a Free Society*, otherwise known as the *Harvard Red Book*. In his letter to the Board of Overseers of Harvard University, James Bryant Conant wrote:

> The heart of the problem of general education is the continuance of the liberal and humane tradition. Neither the mere acquisition of information nor the development of special skills and talents can give the broad basis of understanding which is essential if our civilization is to be preserved.... It includes no history, no art, no literature, no philosophy. Unless the educational process includes at each level of maturity some continuing contact with those fields in which value judgments are of prime importance, it must fall far short of the ideal.... (viii)

A committee of twelve men at an elite university in 1943 wanting to preserve what was a sexist and racist civilization poses its own problems, but their message about the instrumentalization of education at the cost of value judgments resonates today. The concern throughout the *Harvard Red Book* was that the push for job skills would dominate higher education at the expense of the liberal arts. "It has been said that our businessmen, prospecting among school or college graduates for future employees, are chiefly interested in the student's proficiency in activities and not in courses…. The great danger is that there should be two sets of values in the school—intellectual and practical—moving as it were on parallel tracks and never meeting" (Harvard Committee 1943, 172–173). This conviction seems nearly lost. Today, even the liberal arts are conceived of as vocational education. Problematically, so are public sociology and civil society practiced as governance.

The Problem

Public sociology emerged in concert with a renewed emphasis on civil society, which I discuss in Chapter Four, and with observations of a democratic shift toward governance, which I discuss in Chapter Five. All three of these phrases emerged in sync with neoliberalism and its associated governing practices, which I address in Chapters Six and Seven. As Table 1-2 indicates, the circulation of these phrases, which claim to represent transformation, seems to be outpacing transformation of the institutions and practices to which they refer; they seem to be functioning to "discipline imagination" (Agger 1989a, 86) in the absence of public debate by those most impacted by their associated practices.

This spatial representation is not meant to simplify or solidify the contemporary use of the concepts explored in this book, but instead to demonstrate the importance of discerning from multiple uses and meanings the ideals to which their advocates would have us ascribe and to reveal the artificiality of the boundaries that separate them. For example, if we advocate democratic action in civil society, does our use of the phrase *civil society* describe a space distinct from the state where the public engages in critical debate about the actions taken by the state? Or, does *civil society* describe a space within which non-state organizations partner with the state to deliver public services? Would such a partnership, described as governance, eliminate "non-state" space? What would be the implications of such an elimination for governing democratically? Such questions are only a small representation of the challenges posed by the recent emphasis on public sociology and civil society as a means to achieve democratic governance.

I attempt to understand how these phrases, which convey a *sense* of democratic social action, might inhibit our recognition of unnecessarily oppressive power relations embedded in practice as they disguise these practices in the *language* of transformation divorced from the transformation of *practice*. I critically engage the ideals of public sociology, civil society, and governance with the aim of revealing the possibility of a more democratic distribution of power relations, especially those power relations that are structured by knowledge (Foucault 1980; Horkheimer and Adorno 1989). This requires that I acknowledge up front that my argument stems from my preferred

Table 1-2 The Problem

Ontological Claims	Disciplinary References	Institutionalizations	Epistemological Power/Practices
Public Sociology within an Organic Division of Labor	Professional Sociology; Policy Sociology	Nongovernmental organizations (NGOs); Professional academic networks; Publishing norms; The state; Universities	Accountability; Efficiency; Legitimacy by effectiveness; Performance measurement; Positivism
Civil Society	Development Studies; Nonprofit Studies; Political Science; Public Administration and Policy; Sociology	Nongovernmental organizations (NGOs); Professional academic networks; Publishing norms; Foundations; Philanthropy; The state; University centers	Accountability; Efficiency; Legitimacy by effectiveness; Performance measurement
Governance	Development Studies; Management; Nonprofit Studies; Political Science; Public Administration and Policy; Sociology	Nongovernmental organizations (NGOs); Foundations; Intergovernmental organizations (IGOs); Publishing norms; Professional academic networks; The market; The state	Accountability; Efficiency; Legitimacy by effectiveness; Performance measurement

explanation of the world, which might be contested by my readers. The following positions inform my argument and also provide a basis for understanding the underlying intersections of public sociology, civil society, and governance.

Ontology, Epistemology, and Governing

In their shared emphasis on democratic public engagement, public sociology, civil society, and governance seem on the surface to describe similar ideals. Beneath their labels, these ideals are structured by fundamental assumptions about how the world is ordered and "what exists." The idea that there is a boundary between the state, civil society, and the market is based in an ontological assumption that assumes that our experience in the world takes place according to these boundaries. This is a powerful assumption, because these boundaries focus our attention and action; we act "as if" the world is permanently ordered into three spheres; our imagination is governed by this ontological assumption.

Ontology is practiced through portrayal: of a division of labor, of a division between the state and civil society, or of a radical transformation to governance. To the extent that we incorrectly internalize this portrayal as unchangeable, it governs. I understand portrayal to be the rendering of one's view of the world into a medium observable by others (Nickel 2009), such as Burawoy's division of labor in Table 1-1. Although I am focused here on academic portrayals, all renderings of portrayal (architecture, art, literature, music) share at the least the characteristic that the disputes over their renderings are disputes "fought over power and knowledge" (Luke 2002, 220). Portrayals "help to forge reality, and then they organize the collective rites of this unstable reality's reception that will write authoritative accounts of the past, present, and future in their displays" (Luke 2002, 219–220). An underlying assumption in my argument is that advocates of public sociology, civil society, and governance are involved in a common activity: portrayal of the world. Knowledge production is an act of advocating a version of the world and thus it potentially contributes to governing (stabilizing, managing, controlling), because governing depends on most people being accepting of the circumstances of their lives and the factors that produce these circumstances as "social facts rather than literary acts" (Agger 2000).

Of particular concern in this book is the ontology of academic labor, such as it is portrayed by Burawoy in his division of labor, and the way that this interacts with the ontology of the state. A standpoint, such as the standpoint of civil society advanced by Burawoy, is an ontological portrayal. Burawoy has practiced ontological governance in his portrayal of the world as being easily divisible into three spheres—the state, market, and civil society. His (2005a) "organic division of labor" for sociology assumes this ontology and also stabilizes it. It is therefore important as we consider Burawoy's "standpoint of civil society" that we also consider that this standpoint shares its ontology with the state. In his reference to a division between the state, civil society, and the market, he implies that a clear boundary exists and reinforces the idea that governing takes place in a contained space outside of civil society. As I will explain in Chapters Three and Four, the explanation of the shift from government (which is based in a boundary between the state and civil society) to governance (the collapse of this boundary) is therefore an ontological one.

In assuming that governing is limited to the state, Burawoy relies upon and manages the ontological assumption that the world is divided into three spheres, which are *mirrored* in academic disciplines. Agger does not, as Burawoy does, insist on preserving the boundary between sociology and other disciplines. For Agger (1989b) the "assemblage of interdisciplinary knowledge is crucial in order to address a world fragmenting knowledge not only to comply with the alleged inexorability of endless differentiation ... intellectual fragmentation both mirrors, and thereby reproduces, social fragmentation" (78). As Evelyn Nakano Glenn (2007) argues, Burawoy's defense of professional sociology "reflects not only the process of male-dominated professionalization but also the reification of boundaries through the organization of the university, which divides knowledge into discipline-based departments, relegating newer, interdisciplinary fields like ethnic studies and women's studies to the devalued margins" (215). The maintenance of academic disciplines and institutionalizations, themselves ontological boundaries, is an act of governing because these boundaries not only appear to mirror "reality," but also stabilize this reality as they are "received uncritically" (Agger 1989c, 24).

Burawoy's claim on civil society as the providence of sociology demonstrates how difficult it is to break down the supposed boundaries between political science (the state), sociology (civil society), and economics (the market), which produce knowledge "as if" seepage between these spheres does not occur. Even as governance scholars advocate partnership between the state, civil society, and the market, political science, sociology, and economics maintain the academic boundaries that reflect their division. Burawoy's division of labor assumes that social problems take place within the boundaries of academic disciplines and that solutions to these problems can be objectively produced by experts. To propose to cultivate discourse about social problems based on the standpoint of the disciplines limits the scope of such discourse, as Lynd recognized in 1939: "Despite our protestations that everything is interdependent, preoccupation with our specializations tends to put blinkers on us social scientists and to make us state our problems as if they concerned, in fact, isolated economic, or political, or sociological problems" (16). I reject the "standpoint of disciplines" and a culture of expertise, which is a culture in which power is exercised through the authority of knowledge (Foucault 1980; Mitchell 2002).

Following Agger and Timothy W. Luke, I view politics as ontological and ontology as political. I take seriously Luke's (2000) observation that "The progressive teachings of Enlightenment humanism with their strict directives regarding the ontological wrighting of knowledge, resources, and time need to be read as perversely as possible. Dangerous assumptions about living agency are now held so casually that they have acquired virtual invisibility. Unless one takes another interpretive tack, the unearthly propositions of Enlightenment reasoning pull their familiar tricks in any contemporary ontology" (41). Luke's point, like Agger's, is that our assumptions about permanence are now so deeply taken for granted that they have become governors of our imagination about possible alternatives. Reading Agger and Luke, my concern is that public sociology, civil society, and governance might represent degraded ideals, celebrated as alternatives, but failing to recognize that such governing ideals exist in a world that already places epistemological alternatives at large.

I understand ontology and epistemology as mutually reinforcing portrayals. Ontology involves portrayal of the world; epistemology involves portrayal of the possibilities that are inherent to the pursuit of knowledge and its exercise over ontology: What can we know? How much can we know about it? With what certainty can we know it? How objectively can we know it? The more deeply embedded our assumptions about epistemology, the more powerfully it governs action. If we can legitimately know ontological boundaries, claims to the contrary can be dismissed as illegitimate knowledge. If we can know everything that we set out to discover, if we can know with absolute certainty, if we can know without any bias, then once we have employed *the rules that govern the pursuit of knowledge* (Foucault 1972) there is nothing to contest and thus knowledge is not political; all that remains is to render this knowledge into practice—to instrumentalize it as in Burawoy's (2005a) policy sociology. The epistemological possibilities that emerge from "rules of knowledge formation" (Foucault 1972)—disciplinary mechanisms such as Burawoy's (2005a) professional sociology, or publishing norms—are used to authorize and legitimate action. Thus, if it is possible to know, then we have a basis for producing knowledge, and this knowledge itself, discovered and legitimated according to the rules that govern its pursuit, produces its own reason to employ what we know. For example, if we can know a free market to exist (ontology), if we can know human nature to be self-interested, if we can predict human behavior with some certainty based on our normalized professional knowledge of averages (statistics), if we can choose questions objectively, then we are authorized to manage the world according to this knowledge: Welfare benefits can be cut because they are "detrimental to human nature" and "make us lazy"; taxes for the wealthiest in society can be reduced because "economies grow when the wealthy spend" and "the wealthy spend when their taxes are low"; we can declare it impossible to increase the minimum wage because "the data predicts that this will result in higher unemployment."

Although Michel Foucault's work informs parts of this book, in my understanding of epistemology and power I am also building on the work of Max Horkheimer and Theodor Adorno, who were members of what is known as the Frankfurt School. (Foucault labored to explain that he was not a member of any school of thought to which he was assigned.) In *The Dialectic of Enlightenment*, Horkheimer and Adorno (1989) demonstrate how the world portrayed in the image of Enlightenment is one that is infinitely knowable and, as such, can be controlled and governed through instrumental knowledge; this is the practice of knowledge that Burawoy (2005a) preserves for professional and policy sociology. Enlightenment thought is "aimed at liberating men from fear and establishing their sovereignty" (4). Enlightenment thought takes an epistemological position: It makes claims about what is knowable and governs an uncontrolled world through the imposition of this knowledge as fact and as necessity. For Horkheimer and Adorno (1989), like Foucault, "knowledge, which is power, knows no obstacles.... Power and knowledge are synonymous" (4).

In Parts I and II, I attempt to locate the ontological claims of public sociology, civil society, and governance and their institutionalization as instrumental knowledge. In Part III, I demonstrate that, in practice, public sociology, civil society, and governance share one epistemology, which has failed to break with the Enlightenment view of knowledge as an instrumental tool for operationalizing and exploiting nature; this is evidenced in Burawoy's (2005a) reservation of instrumental knowledge for "policy" and "professional" sociology.

Affirmative and Critical Intellectuality

The distinction between *professional* and *public* intellectuals neglects that professional intellectuals and instrumental knowledge are equally involved in influencing the public (Agger 1989a, b, c, 2000). I therefore distinguish instead between affirmative and critical intellectuals in order to reveal how an intellectual's view of knowledge production and its synchronicity with the present relates to governing. Intellectuals can be understood to have an affirmative or critical relationship to the *present* (ontology), an affirmative or critical position on *knowledge* (epistemology), and an affirmative or critical relationship to *governing* (power/practice). Although there is certainly a degree of disagreement among them, critical theorists today generally view the *present* as something to be changed, whereas affirmative theorists generally view the present as something to be stabilized; critical theorists today generally view *knowledge* as consisting of contestable statements situated within power relations, whereas affirmative theorists today generally view knowledge as consisting of objective facts derived from detached observation; critical theorists generally view contemporary *governing* as a complex and powerful relationship among capitalism, knowledge, and ideology, whereas affirmative theorists generally view contemporary governing as a basically democratic expression of individual interests, administered according to legitimate knowledge.

Sociology began as an affirmative intellectuality known as positivism. Auguste Comte, in the wake of the drastic social upheaval of the French Revolution, wrote of the need for intellectuals—sociologists—to contribute to social cohesion. Positivism in this period, as Comte characterized it, involved a society that would be based not on individual reason, Marx's ideal, but on professional science and the separation of theory and practice. Sociology, for Comte (1988), would endeavor to remedy the omission of "social physics" from the study of *natural* phenomena. "Now that the human mind has founded celestial physics, terrestrial physics (mechanical and chemical), or organic physics (vegetable and animal), it only remains to complete the system of observational sciences by the foundation of social physics" (13).

Thus, sociology at its founding was to be an "observational science" involving the impartial discovery of facts. Positivism, as Comte theorized it, rejected the idea that human beings could imagine and create alternative forms of social organization. For Comte (1969), theorizing the best society was "absurd" because the "individual consciousness" of the people, their ability to think freely in order to change society based on their aspirations, could only result in social unrest; the point was not to change society, but to stabilize it through the discovery of social laws. "In astronomy, physics, chemistry and physiology there is no such thing as liberty of conscience; that is to say, everyone would deem it absurd not to place confidence in the principles established for these sciences by competent thinkers" (1969, 250). The task for sociology according to this view was to determine the scientific principles of society: the laws according to which we would be governed.

Marx's eleventh thesis in his 1845 *Theses on Feuerbach* broke with this tradition. "The philosophers have only interpreted the world in various ways; the point is to change it." Marx's oft-quoted statement, which figures prominently in both Agger's and Burawoy's conceptions of public sociology, was radical not only because of its declaration that intellectuals *ought* to change the world (radicalize knowledge to unleash transformative potential of the present), but also because of the recognition that intellectuals *do* change the world (knowledge is *always* political). Marx did not suddenly inspire intellectuals to be political; both affirmative and critical intellectuals were already political. What is revolutionary about Marx's statement is not his call for influencing society, but his recognition of *the contestability* of the ideas that intellectuals circulate in their creation of meaning. As a theorist concerned with how ideas govern actions, Marx was calling for intellectuals to reveal alternative understandings of what exists, which would in turn reveal alternative courses of action as being debatable by those whose lives such actions impact. The contrast between positivism and Marxism is summarized by Agger and Luke (2002):

> Positivism is a version of the social sciences modeled on the natural sciences, promising cause-and-effect understandings of social life. Marx breaks with positivism, because he views the person as an agent, responsible for her own fate, albeit within limits imposed by history, politics, economics, family, gender, race. Marxism is not deterministic. People are free to change their history, effecting social change made possible by a combination of free will or agency and propitious social and economic circumstances for revolutionary intervention … it resists the metaphysical, as opposed to empirical, conclusion that people's lives are simply predetermined by forces that are as implacable as the tides, gravity, space and time. (168–169)

Nearly fifty years after Marx's thesis, Emile Durkheim (1933) was still arguing on behalf of scientific social facts, claiming that society was something to be *described* by professional sociologists, but not something to be *changed* by public sociologists. In *The Division of Labor in Society* Durkheim (1933) wrote of sociological investigations and epistemology:

> We must be careful to admit no explanation that does not rest on authentic proofs. The methods we have used in giving the greatest possible exactness will thus be judged. To subject an order of facts to science, it is not sufficient to observe them carefully, to describe and classify them, but what is a great deal more difficult, we must find, in the words of Descartes, *the way in which they are scientific* … to discover in them some objective element that allows an exact determination, and if possible, measurement. (37)

It was this version of professional sociology that Agger opposed in the years up to his call for public sociology. Durkheim, Agger (1989b) argued, "charted sociology as the discourse of subordination, endlessly reflecting—and thus fatefully reproducing—the power of the social. *Fact*—capitalism, patriarchy, racism, the domination of nature—thus becomes *fate* …" (3).

The success of the positivist tradition in the United States can be credited in large part to the professional success of U.S. sociologist Talcott Parsons at Harvard University from 1927 to 1973. As Clyde Barrow (1987) pointed out, for Parsons the intellectual was an "ideal-type … politically autonomous critic pursuing knowledge for its own sake" (415). The claims of the autonomous intellectual as an ideal type, Barrow (1987) contends, institutionalized "a conceptual distinction between those intellectuals committed to a course of social or political action and those committed to 'scientific objectivity'" (421). This same distinction is employed by Burawoy when he distinguishes between ideal-type professional, public, policy, and critical sociologists. Burawoy, as Gouldner (1970) observed of Comte and Parsons, employs "taxonomic zeal, crudely utilizing four-fold tables [or planes] as a logic machine to chop out mountains of conceptual distinctions" (205). Echoing positivism's imitation of the physical sciences, Burawoy charts a new social physics to which politics conforms. The intellectual as an ideal-type has political implications because it legitimates the "facts" chosen by intellectuals for observation *as such* because they were observed by intellectuals who have chosen to identify themselves as objectively and factually autonomous. As they become institutionalized, these facts are then rendered into practice.

These different styles of intellectuality—affirmative and critical—stem from a thinker's *telos*—their intent or purpose in portraying the world in a particular way. Styles of intellectuality conform to a particular stance on knowledge, or epistemology. Positivism was affirmative in the sense that it sought to prevent social change through the "scientific" determination of social laws, resting on "authentic proofs," which could then be used to portray the present as natural. In contrast, critical intellectuality seeks to reveal how these facts are a matter of choice and how the present is politically ordered and therefore could be ordered differently.

Although I have chosen the labels *affirmative* and *critical,* many theorists before me have distinguished between types of intellectuals. In the critical tradition, Gramsci (1997), circa 1930, distinguished between "traditional intellectuals" and "organic intellectuals." Traditional intellectuals, like Parsons's intellectuals, are autonomous. Organic intellectuals "know" based on the everyday experiences of the groups to which they belong and use this knowledge to "change the world," as Marx recommended. From the view of the organic intellectual, the knowledge inherent to life as a factory worker in capitalist industrial society—knowledge about alienation, poverty, degradation—is not only legitimate, but also can be *transformed into a critique of the present* by organic intellectuals from every strata of society. Economists might explain your level of well-being as being the result of your individual abilities combined with your chosen level of effort in a basically fair economic system. However, you might know otherwise, by virtue of having exercised your abilities within an economic system that offers no opportunities. Your experience can be translated into a critique of the economic system that portrays your low level of well-being as resulting from your lack of effort, rather than as the result of socioeconomic arrangements that have been portrayed as "facts" that cannot be altered, such as "healthy" or "cyclical" levels of unemployment.

When asked about the role of intellectuals in political struggles, Foucault (1980) distinguished between universal and specific intellectuals (125–126). The universal intellectual, like the traditional intellectual, was the "spokesman of the universal," autonomous from the politics within which he or she was situated. The specific intellectual, like the organic intellectual, works at the "precise points where their own conditions of life or work situate them (housing, the hospital, the asylum, the laboratory, the university, family and sexual relations)" (126). Foucault's (1980) point that specific intellectuals are subject to power relations is an important one: "It has been a question of real, material, everyday struggles ... [intellectuals] have often been confronted, albeit in a different form, by the same adversary as the proletariat, namely the multinational corporations, the judicial and police apparatuses, the property speculators ..." (126). The "ivory tower" intellectual, who is blissfully unaware of the conditions of everyday life, if he or she ever existed, would be the exception to the rule today. Today intellectuals are situated within a market that often allows, but also often requires, them to work independent of the patronage that supported traditional intellectuals, such as the clergy noted by Gramsci. Intellectuals live and work in "the real world," often with significant student loan debt and relatively low salaries, if they are lucky enough to be employed at all (Nickel 2008). Foucault might be overly optimistic, however, about the increasing solidarity between intellectuals and the proletariat. Today intellectuals are encouraged, if not required as a condition of employment, to seek patrons in the form of foundations and governments to pay for the production of positivist knowledge, a point that I return to in Part II.

Although I find the distinction between affirmative and critical intellectuality important, I caution that building typologies of intellectuals has the potential to digress from the act of making critical distinctions, as Gramsci and Foucault did, to the act of distracting us from the intent of these distinctions, which is to transform intellectuality, not to put it in a box. Political scientist and public intellectual Theodore J. Lowi (2010), in what might be interpreted as a wry tone, calls attention to the intellectual types employed by Amitati Etzioni in his autobiography: the public intellectual (PI), the private intellectual (PrI), the alienated intellectual (AI), the government intellectual (GI), and the movement intellectual (MI). Although I cannot speak to Lowi's (2010) intended tone, his discussion struck me as perhaps a bit flippant: "Now that I have uncovered at least three types of intellectuals already [in the first three paragraphs of the article], I will need designations for quick comparison.... [Etzioni] had moved from UI to PI and from PI to AI and on to GI ..." (675). Although many scholars, such as Burawoy, take their typology-building quite seriously, it is important to keep in mind that the reason for making distinctions between types of intellectuals is to uncover their relation to governing practices.

What the critical intellectuals discussed in this book share in common is the recognition that all intellectuals are involved in the production of understanding and that, to the extent that this understanding discourages critical reflection, it functions as what Marx called ideology, Gramsci (1997) called hegemony, Georg Lukacs (1968) called reification, Horkheimer and Adorno (1989) called domination, Herbert Marcuse (1964) called one-dimensionality, and Foucault (1995) called discipline. *Ideology, reification, hegemony, domination, one-dimensionality,* and *discipline* are words that describe the way in which ideas about present relations of power are taken for granted as natural and, thus, not only do we not oppose them, we make personal choices that further embed them in our everyday lives. These ideas are communicated not only by governments, but through schools, economic relations and labor, the culture industry (Horkheimer and Adorno 1989), and professions such as psychiatry (Foucault 1973). They are also institutionalized by intellectuals in their ontological claims and epistemological practices.

Critical Theory and Conceptual Significance

It is not an uncomplicated task to consider together public sociology, civil society, and governance and their relationship to politics and power. In its emphasis on the political relationship between knowledge and governing and their implications for the distribution of power, critical theory is uniquely suited for this task. *Critical theory,* a phrase originating in the work of Max Horkheimer (1972) and framing the work of the Frankfurt School, recognizes the need to politicize ontologies and the knowledge that stabilizes them, thus exposing them as the temporary narratives that they are. It does so while recognizing that these foundations are still empirically functioning and thus must be reformulated. To politicize ontology and epistemology is a matter of "isolating the status of the one-and-only reason, in order to show that it is only *one* possible form among others" (Foucault 1998, 441). As Agger (1993) notes, critical theory: "functions in everyday life as the activity of critique sensitizing us to the ways in which what Foucault calls discourse/practices cast a certain politically immobilizing spell over us and pointing beyond the present toward a future in which discourse deconstructs itself..." (26). (See also Benhabib 1986; Calhoun 1995; Fraser 1989; Kellner 1989; Luke 1989a.)

My stance toward public sociology, civil society, and governance as governing language draws extensively on Agger's (1989a) critical theory of significance. As Table 1-2 demonstrates, it is increasingly difficult to discern what it is that we are talking about when we talk about public sociology, civil society, or governance. These concepts signify so many competing ideals and activities that they fail to signify at all. Agger (1989a) criticized this trend as a symptom of what he calls "fast capitalism," which "degrades every concept quickly, celebrating its novelty and then dispersing it to name things that live as a parody of what [the] concept was initially meant to criticize" (84). When public sociologists advocate governance through NGOs, when NGOs do the work of government, and when governments enthusiastically institutionalize a space called civil society, which simultaneously is claimed as the standpoint of sociology (Burawoy 2005a), these concepts lose their ability to represent the possibility for transformation (Agger 1989a).

At issue in this collapse of concepts is a central question of critical theory: Fredric Jameson's (1998) "change without its opposite" (52). The transformation of phrases (and their ontological claims) without the transformation of epistemology rendered into practice is an act of governing through what Luke (1990) and Paul Piccone (1978) described as artificial negativity: stabilization of the present through the generation of the appearance of resistance. The phrases *public sociology, civil society,* and *governance* appear to signify opposition to the present, while representing, through these phrases, the present as being oppositional. In other words, transformation seems to be under way, but often it is a transformation in vocabulary unaccompanied by a transformation in practice.

The Argument So Far

My argument thus far has been that *public sociology, civil society,* and *governance* are related terms that can be understood together through an inquiry into the politics of knowledge. It follows that in order to understand the actuality of these declarations, it is first necessary to understand them as epistemological practices in relationship to the requirements of governing. In the remainder of the book, I demonstrate how public sociology and civil society have become institutionalized along the same lines as governance, which is itself the institutionalization of a particular relation of power practiced as an instrumental orientation toward knowledge. Thus, these three portrayals, or ontological claims, become institutionalized along the same powerful line of epistemological practice. This has implications for the democratization of governing toward which all three ideals claim to aspire. To the extent that calls for public sociology, civil society, and governance are focused exclusively on making ontological claims rather than investigating epistemological practices, they neglect a major conduit of power relations.

Part I

The Politics of Knowledge

No, I'd say: I'd swear
that men have always lounged in myths
as Tall Stories

—*W. H. Auden*, Archaeology, *1973*

Chapter 2

Public Sociology

Locating the Argument

Since Burawoy's 2004 Presidential Address to the ASA, his idea of public sociology has resonated through a symphony of professional journal symposia, conference proceedings, and newsletters, has been translated in twelve languages, and has even been made available in video. With Burawoy's stewardship, public sociology was promoted as the topic of at least six journal symposia between 2004 and 2008, to which he contributed: *Social Problems* (2004a, b), *Social Forces* (2004c), *Critical Sociology* (2005c), *British Journal of Sociology* (2005b), *Socio-Economic Review* (2007c), and *Current Sociology* (2008). Additionally, Burawoy participated in least four edited books dedicated to his argument, including *The Public Sociologies Reader* (Blau and Smith 2006), *Public Sociology: The Contemporary Debate* (Nichols 2007), *Public Sociology: Fifteen Eminent Sociologists Debate Politics and the Profession in the Twenty-First Century* (Clawson, et al. 2007), and *Handbook of Public Sociology* (Jeffries 2009).

The rapid production of arguments for and against public sociology, and Burawoy's involvement in nearly all of them, has resulted in a confusing array of statements as he has attempted to accommodate his critics and absorb their arguments into his vision of an "organic" public sociology (2005a). Six years after his initial campaign, Burawoy has claimed for public sociology such a wide array of topics that the intellectual practice of sociology would have to involve the reconciliation of completely incompatible positions, epistemologies, and ontologies. In this chapter I attempt to temporally and substantively locate these often contradictory arguments and their institutionalization along the lines of the instrumental rationality of governing.

The Campaign for Public Sociology

The contemporary campaign for public sociology begins in 2004 with the run up to Burawoy's 2005 Presidential Address. As Craig Calhoun (2005) wrote, "Michael Burawoy's Presidential Address to the 2005[1] ASA meeting was an extraordinary event. There was a buzz of excitement, the culmination of a week of high energy discussions of 'public sociology', and the product also of a year in which Burawoy had criss-crossed the USA speaking to dozens of groups and urging those who often give the ASA a pass in favour of local or activist meetings to come to San Francisco.... 'Public sociology' was a hit" (355). Calhoun's description of the public sociology campaign is no exaggeration; keeping track of Burawoy's campaign for public sociology is quite difficult!

From a publication standpoint, the trail appears to begin with a symposium at Boston College in April 2003. Following the symposium, in February 2004 *Social Problems* published "Public Sociologies: A Symposium from Boston College," which is introduced by Burawoy (2004a) and includes his "Manifesto for Public Sociologies" (2004b) and responses written by invited symposium participants. In June 2004, following the North Carolina Sociological Association meetings in March 2004, *Social Forces* would publish a debate on public sociologies, including Burawoy's "Public Sociologies: Contradictions, Dilemmas, and Possibilities" and invited responses. These two publications by Burawoy (2004b, 2004c) would subsequently evolve into the ASA Presidential Address, *For Public Sociology*, in 2005. To my knowledge, the address is published in *American Sociological Review* (2005a) and the *British Journal of Sociology* (2005b) and again in an edited book published in 2007 and titled *Public Sociology: Fifteen Eminent Sociologists Debate Politics and the Profession in the Twenty-First Century* (Burawoy 2007a). All four of the articles (2004b, 2004c, 2005a, 2005b) include Burawoy's division of labor.

The division of labor is first mentioned in Burawoy's (2005c) Critical Turn essay, where the intent is clearly stated to be the preservation of sociology *against* radicalization: "Let me be clear, our disciplinary project cannot and should not be reduced to *critical sociology*, which makes no sense without a *professional sociology* to criticize or even without a *public sociology* to infuse with its commitments, just as all three find their complement in a *policy sociology* with its more instrumental deployment of knowledge" (318). This initial statement is then further elaborated in each subsequent essay and reflected in Burawoy's boxes, within which he places the function of public sociology. In 2005 *Critical Sociology* published a symposium discussing Burawoy's (2005c) "The Critical Turn to Public Sociology," which first appeared in 2004 as a chapter in *Enriching the Sociological Imagination: How Radical Sociology Changed the Discipline* (Levine 2004) and thus, although published again later in *Critical Sociology*, was written before the 2004 address. In 2006 Burawoy would elaborate on his argument in "A Public Sociology for Human Rights," which served as the introduction to the *Public Sociologies Reader.* Next, a 2006 address delivered in Beijing would evolve into Burawoy's (2007c) 2007 publication of "Public Sociology vs. The Market" in *Socio-Economic Review*'s discussion forum, titled "Economic Sociology as Public Sociology." In 2008 *Current Sociology* published Burawoy's (2008) statement, "What Is To Be Done? Theses on the Degradation of Social Existence in a Globalizing World," which makes the same substantive argument as the 2006 and 2007 publications, that third-wave marketization requires a response from public sociology.

Although the publication trail of Burawoy's promotion of public sociology is difficult to follow, the evolution of the substantive argument over three years is even more so. The argument seems to evolve in three phases, each with a distinct definition of public sociology. The first phase, including the ASA Presidential Address and the division of labor that I explained in the Introduction, defined public sociology as one of four "species" within the discipline.

The second phase, which I explore further in Chapter Seven, is "a public sociology for human rights," which first appeared in the *Public Sociologies Reader* in 2006, where Burawoy argued that (2006) "the advantage of a human rights framework is its widespread appeal. Who, after all, can be against human rights?" (5). If the topics in the *Reader* are an indication, public sociology for human rights includes many interdisciplinary themes: governance, globalization, and cosmopolitanism (also see Beck 2005b and Sassen 2009), the rights of humans, sustainability and peace, utopia, feminism (which has always been a form of public sociology), and challenges to neoliberalism. The third phase of Burawoy's campaign begins with his 2007 publication of "Public Sociology vs. The Market" in *Socio-Economic Review*'s discussion forum titled "Economic Sociology as Public Sociology" (2007c) and his publication of "Third Wave Sociology" (2007d), in Lawrence T. Nichols's *Public Sociology: The Contemporary Debate.* (Many of the papers in this book appeared earlier as a symposium published in 2005 in *The American Sociologist,* also edited by Nichols.) This third phase involves public sociology as political economy, which, Burawoy argues, should resist what he, echoing Karl Polanyi, calls "third-wave marketization" and neoliberalism. This phase continued into 2009 with "Public Sociology in the Age of Obama" (Burawoy 2009b).

It is difficult to treat Burawoy's argument for public sociology as a comprehensive and internally consistent statement, but it is possible to identify an underlying thesis and then parse out the varying portrayals used to support it. Although his definition of public sociology varies, Burawoy (2004d) has advanced one thesis: "the world needs public sociology." This thesis is constructed through what I identify as two supporting portrayals, which Burawoy (2005a) argues are necessary because there is a "growing gap between the sociological ethos and the world we study" (4). These two portrayals, which are based in ontological assumptions that I reject in the remainder of the book, are that there exists a division of sociological labor and that there exists a clear boundary between civil society, the state, and the market.

Portrayal One: The Existence of a Division of Sociological Labor

I identify the existence of a division of sociological labor as Burawoy's (2005a) first of two portrayals because it this division, not the normative impetus to which he gives vague reference, that is his basis for theorizing public sociology as an intellectual function. Though he provides reasons independent of a division of labor for why public sociology is necessary, he does not theorize public sociology independent of a division of sociological labor and, in fact, argues that there can be no public sociology without such a division (10). In other words, the division of sociological labor is Burawoy's normative stance on the functions of sociological labor and is thus an argument for his specific hierarchical organization of the functions of professional, policy, and critical sociology as much as it is an argument "for public sociology." All divisions of labor are, of course, normative portrayals of social organization; labor could be organized differently (see Rothschild 1979, 2000). Though Burawoy (2005a) explains in some detail what his division of labor for sociology entails, he says surprisingly little about the fact that his division of labor, not only his call for public sociology, is a decidedly political statement, not a natural intellectual order. There is a *negotiable* boundary inherent in our statements about the naturalness of who does what and why.

In this first portrayal, Burawoy (2005a) is careful to distinguish his vision of "organic public sociology" from what he calls the "traditional public sociology." "The traditional public sociologist instigates debates within or between publics, although he or she might not actually participate in them" (Burawoy 2005a, 7). The organic public sociologist "works in close connection with a visible, thick, active, local, and often counterpublic" (7). This distinction, which reflects Gramsci's distinction between traditional and organic intellectuals, which I discussed in the Introduction, is not problematic at first glance. Like Agger (2000), Burawoy (2005a) argues that organic public sociologists will turn the public's private troubles into public issues "by engaging their lives not suspending them; *starting from where they are, not from where we are*" (9, my emphasis). However, two paragraphs later, Burawoy argues that public sociology must originate from where "we" are: "C. Wright Mills (1959), and many others since him, would turn all sociology into public sociology. Mills harks back to the late 19th century forefathers, for whom scholarly and moral enterprises were indistinguishable. There is no turning back, however, to that earlier period before academic revolution. Instead we have to move forward and *work from where we really are, from the division of sociological labor*" (9, my emphasis).

It is unclear how a division of labor for sociology that preserves professional sociology is a solution to traditional public sociology's failure to engage fully with the public. Preserving professional sociology has very little to do with encouraging a more organic intellectuality; in fact, as I demonstrate in Chapter Three, it is possible that it does exactly the opposite. It seems reasonable to ask, what is going on here? First, Burawoy is correct that traditional public sociologists would turn all sociology into public sociology. This poses a problem for him, because it challenges the legitimacy of professional sociology, which he intends to preserve. Not intending to challenge the legitimacy of professional sociology, Burawoy (2005a) therefore frames traditional public sociology as flawed because it was inorganic in Gramsci's sense of organic intellectuals. Although the same criticism would have to be directed at professional sociology, he exempts professional sociology from criticism because its "function" within the division of labor is not "public." Burawoy is therefore able to protect professional sociology from the challenge posed by "traditional public sociology." He then uses the division of labor, which he claims is "organic," to reconstruct "organic public sociology." The result is that Burawoy employs the supposed failures of previous public sociologists to legitimate the failures of current professional sociologists.

Organic public sociology framed in this way is less about working with publics and more about absorbing the failures of professional sociology into a division of labor, portraying these failures as "where we really are" with "no possibility of turning back." Organic public sociology, as Burawoy has defined it, thus makes it possible to preserve the discipline "as it is" based on his assertion that Mills was not an organic public sociologist. (See Aronowitz 2003 for a discussion of Mills's career.) According to this logic, we have two alternatives: the "failed" intellectuality of previous "traditional public sociologists" *or* the intellectuality of the present, which is preserved by Burawoy's division of labor. We can either treat the public as "invisible," as he asserts that traditional public sociologists did, or we can accept the organic division of labor that legitimates the "revolution" that professionalized sociology, which is guilty at least of the same failures as traditional public sociology, but absolved by its "function" within a division of labor. Burawoy (2005a) has neglected a significant alternative, which is to transform traditional public sociology into organic public sociology, while retaining the critique of professional sociology and the call to transform all sociology into organic public sociology. In other words, if the failure of traditional public sociology was a failure to engage in organic public sociology, then the solution would not be to preserve professional sociology in a division of labor "from where we are" in order to "engage the public not from where we are, but from where they are." Certainly, traditional public sociology could be improved through a more organic style of public sociology. However, the solution to traditional public sociology is not preserving professional sociology through a division of labor; if traditional public sociology failed to engage the public, the solution would be to engage in organic public sociology instead of traditional public sociology.

Portrayal Two: The Existence of a Boundary Between Civil Society, the State, and the Market

The second portrayal in Burawoy's argument for public sociology is constructed in the second and third phases in the intersection of Burawoy's (2006) "A Public Sociology for Human Rights," "Public Sociology vs. The Market," (2007c), and "What Is To Be Done?" (2008), in which he relies less on the division of labor as the defining principle of public sociology and more upon a division between civil society, the state, and the market. In "A Public Sociology for Human Rights," public sociology is defined by Burawoy (2006) as the defense of human rights against markets and states, although both philanthropic markets (Nickel and Eikenberry 2007) and states also claim to defend human rights. Rather than basing public sociology in a division of labor, here Burawoy (2006) bases public sociology in relation to capitalism and its "three sets of institutions": the market economy, the liberal state, and civil society (6). Public sociology positioned in relationship to the market, as opposed to Burawoy's earlier case for public sociology positioned in relationship to professional, critical, and policy sociology, is further elaborated in "Public Sociology vs. The Market," where Burawoy (2007c), who claims to be building on the work of Karl Polanyi, argues that there have been three waves of marketization—labor, money, and land—and three waves of sociology—utopian, policy, and public. "Sociology has to take a public turn. Sociology lives and dies with society. When society is threatened, so is sociology. We can no longer rely on the state to contain the market and so sociologists have to forge their own connections to society, i.e. to develop public sociology. We have to do more than passively serve society, but have to conserve and constitute society" (Burawoy 2007c, 366).

Whereas in the first portrayal Burawoy relied upon clear boundaries between professional, policy, critical, and public sociology, in this second portrayal, Burawoy (2005a) relies upon clear boundaries between civil society, the state, and the market in order to distinguish sociology from other disciplines on the basis of what he claims is sociology's unique claim to civil society, "if the standpoint of economics is the market and its expansion, and the standpoint of political science is the state and the guarantee of political stability, then the standpoint of sociology is civil society and the defence of the social. In times of market tyranny and state despotism, sociology—and in particular its public face—defends the interests of humanity" (24). This boundary reinforces the knowledge boundary that he has constructed in his division of labor, where he distinguished between instrumental knowledge (produced by professional and policy sociology and employed in the state and the market) and reflexive knowledge (produced by critical and public sociology and employed in civil society). This boundary assumes not only that the instrumental knowledge produced by the state and the market has no impact on the possibility of reflexive knowledge in civil society, but also that knowledge reflects the division of academic disciplines, and therefore, instrumental knowledge produced by professional and policy sociology is somehow different from the instrumental knowledge produced by political science and economics.

The standpoint of civil society, as Burawoy has implied it, assumes a distinction among three sectors—the state, market, and civil society. Burawoy (2006) reproduces this distinction as disciplinary divisions in academia, holding political science (the state) and economics (the market) responsible for the advance of neoliberalism, while absolving sociology of contributing to social problems because, he argues, the standpoint of sociology is civil society, which keeps its distance from the state and the market (8). On the basis of this claim, Burawoy (2006) goes so far as to blame the public-sector emphasis on political science and economics over sociology for no less than tyranny and despotism, arguing that sociologists "have to maintain the integrity of sociology's critical standpoint, namely civil society, in the face of challenges from economists and political scientists who are largely responsible for ideologies justifying the collusion of market tyranny and state despotism" (17).

In advancing the standpoint of civil society, Burawoy (2006) relies upon what Neera Chandhoke (2002) called the three sector fallacy, "contemporary thinking gives us a picture of global civil society that seems to be supremely uncontaminated by either the power of states or that of markets" (36). Chandhoke (2001) recognizes how this ontological assumption of three independent spheres is further reinforced by the assumption of knowledge boundaries, such as Burawoy's (2005a) boundary between instrumental and reflexive knowledge, which "also throws up the additional problem of how overlapping boundaries can possibly contain separate and discrete logics.... [C]an we think of *any* sphere of human activity as either autonomous or as marked by a different logic?" (Chandhoke 2001, 6).

As I will explore further in Chapters Four and Seven, Burawoy's (2006, 2007c) argument for *autonomous* public sociology positioned against the market and the state is deeply problematic. As I will explain in Part II, among theorists of the state, there is little agreement about what the state is, where its boundaries are, how the state functions, and whether there is a state at all, or a "political system" instead (see Mitchell 1991). The boundary between the market, the liberal state, and civil society, like the boundary between intellectual role categories, is not as clean as Burawoy (2006, 2007c) theorizes it to be. Even if these spheres existed, it would remain empirically untrue that sociology is autonomous from either the market or the state (see Barrow 1990; Gouldner 1970; Mills 2000). The growth of sociology following World War II, Alvin Gouldner (1970) argues, was fueled by the growth of the welfare state (161). "Above all, what one sees is a vast growth in the demand for *applied* social science: the *policy*-oriented use of social science by governments, both for welfare and warfare purposes …" (Gouldner 1970, 345).

Public Sociology, the Public Interest, and the Secular Spirit

In Burawoy's early campaign for public sociology, he argues that sociology has an inherent public purpose, discussed variously by Burawoy as "the moral impetus behind sociology" (2004b, 124), "sociological ethos" (2004c, 1604), and the "original passion for social justice, economic equality, human rights, sustainable environment, political freedom or simply a better world" (2005a, 5). Public administration scholars will recognize Burawoy's ethical impetus theme as reminiscent of New Public Administration (Frederickson 1980) or New Public Service (Denhardt and Denhardt 2003):

- **New public administration:** "Simply put, new public administration seeks to change those policies and structures that systematically inhibit social equity" (Frederickson 1980, 8).
- **New public service:** "Public service itself is seen as an extension of citizenship, motivated by desire to serve others and to achieve public objectives" (Denhardt and Denhardt 2003, 170).
- **Public sociology:** "A sociology that seeks to bring sociology to publics beyond the academy, promoting dialogue about issues that affect the fate of society, placing the values to which we adhere under a microscope" (Burawoy 2004a, 104).

Like Burawoy, public administration scholars and, as I will discuss in Chapter Four, political scientists, sought to "achieve the public interest" through the organization and reorganization of labor.

In spite of this claim to the "public interest," Burawoy's division of labor reflects what political scientist and public administration scholar Dwight Waldo (1948) criticized as the "secular spirit" (23). Divisions of labor such as Burawoy's, like public administration circa 1900 (see Goodnow 1900), are uncritical manifestations of Max Weber's *critical* idea of the ideal type bureaucracy as officialdom, of which functional specialization is one characteristic. Burawoy (2004c) claims that "like Weber, I believe that without value commitments there can be no sociology, no basis for the questions that guide our research programs…. We should try to be clear about those values by engaging in what Weber called value discussion, leading to what I will refer to as *reflexive knowledge*" (1606). However, Burawoy's division of labor, which preserves instrumental knowledge, neglects Weber's (2007) observation that the "individual bureaucrat cannot squirm out of the apparatus into which he has been harnessed. In contrast to the 'notable' performing administrative tasks as a honorific duty or as a subsidiary occupation (avocation), the professional bureaucrat is chained to his activity.... In the great majority of cases he is only a small cog in a ceaselessly moving mechanism which prescribes him to an essentially fixed route of march" (272). I suspect that Weber would consider it unlikely that low-ranking professional and policy sociologists assigned a role as instrumental knowledge producers within Burawoy's bureaucracy could squirm their way out of their fixed route of march and into the reflexive quadrants.

Reorganization of labor was a defining characteristic of the rationalization of organizational life that accompanied the demands of industrialization. It is thus useful to read Burawoy's reorganization of sociological labor through the same lens that Waldo read the "Reorganizers." In his discussion of the "Rationalism of Reorganization" Waldo (1948) observed that:

> "Reorganizers," despite the fact that occasionally they are politically crafty in their choice of argument, exhibit as a general rule the impatience and optimism of all reformism.... They are convinced not only of their rightness, but that ... when the advantages of reorganization are explained, [we] will desire as a matter of course the new and superior arrangement.... The Reorganizers stand "outside" their material, seek to impose rational principles upon it, and are inclined to believe that accomplishing their reforms will follow easily upon manipulating their concepts. (37)

Burawoy's (2005a) specialization of sociology was addressed by Waldo in 1948, when he wrote of the field of public administration as being emergent from the tendency toward functional expertise—bureaucratization:

> The course which American study of public administration has taken is also a function of the very great increase in specialization which has featured [in] our recent national life; particularly the rise of American scholarship and the growth of professional spirit and organizations. The fissiparous tendencies of specialization have made more difficult the integration of our national life.... The rise of American scholarship, the spread of a guild spirit among scholars, and the rise of the professional schools have been a part of the general movement towards specialization.... (9–10)

This 1948 observation of the movement toward academic specialization and professional organization is easily extended to Burawoy's industrial-style division of labor, which, though reserving two boxes for reflexive thought, *is itself an act of rational reorganization* of the sort that Waldo was concerned with in 1948. Reflexive public thought for Burawoy (2005a) belongs to a *rational specialization stemming from the secular spirit.*

Critical public administration scholarship (see the journal *Administrative Theory and Praxis*) has, for the most part, recognized since Waldo's 1948 thesis that *a division of labor constitutes political theory.* What Waldo referred to as the politics-administration dichotomy is reincarnated in Burawoy's (2005a) division between political (public) and nonpolitical (professional) knowledge, which depoliticizes professional sociology by assigning *the* political task to public sociology as though all other knowledge is not political. As Waldo (1948) recognized, the distinction between political and nonpolitical knowledge constitutes a false dichotomy, because there is no such thing as knowledge that does not theorize and thus constitute the world (see Agger 1989b). Burawoy's (2005a) argument that academic labor must be reorganized according to functional specialization is thus a political statement reflective of his stance on the politics of knowledge and the public.

Although he has argued for reflexive knowledge, the subtext of Burawoy's (2005a) boxes indicates that he views sociological knowledge as appropriately dichotomized into value-free (professional and policy) and value-laden (public and critical) knowledge. This is the false dichotomy rejected by Waldo (1948) as inappropriate for a scholastic endeavor regarding the well-being of the public: "[Any social science] is concerned primarily with *human beings,* a type of being characterized by *thinking* and *valuing.* Valuing implies morality, conceptions of right and wrong. *It is submitted that the established techniques of science are inapplicable to thinking and valuing human beings*" (181). I thus submit Burawoy's (2005a) reservation for the supposed "science of the social" to a professional quadrant charged with "theoretical/empirical knowledge, correspondent truth, legitimacy by scientific norms, accountability to peers" (16) to Waldo's (1948) statement that "these questions of value are not amenable to scientific treatment.... If mechanical cause and effect obtained in the realm of human affairs no one would *need* to tell the government what to do; what it does would be predetermined, fixed, and invariable" (182). For Waldo, Burawoy's (2005a) division of labor, with its emphasis on professional and policy sociology, seems to render through professional sociology a public sociology that is wholly unnecessary except as the voice of sociological legitimacy and relevance.

During the period that Waldo was writing, circa 1950, sociologists, too, were concerned with the bureaucratization of knowledge. C. Wright Mills (2000) described the transformation of sociology into a "bureaucratic social science": "'the new social science' has come to serve whatever ends its bureaucratic clients may have in view. Those who promote and practice this style of research readily assume the political perspective of their bureaucratic clients.... In so far as such research efforts are effective in their declared practical aims, they serve to increase the efficiency and the reputation—and to that extent, the prevalence—of bureaucratic forms of domination in modern society" (101). The turn to bureaucratic uses of knowledge concerned Mills because it resulted in a "sociologist of applied research," who was less inclined to address "the public" (Mills uses quotation marks with this phrase), preferring instead to address a client (102). Importantly, this client now, as it was when Mills was writing, is often the state, which draws upon for legitimacy what Agger (1989c) calls the "science aura"—or the falsely apparent objectivity of sociological "facts." If particular modes of governing and economy require a particular mode of knowing in order to legitimize social organization, then sociology is able to govern public imagination in both stabilizing and transformative ways (Gouldner 1970).

We can thus view Burawoy's (2005a) division of labor as the "rationalization" of the discipline of sociology, but not only sociology; in his decision to reorganize and structure specialized academic labor, Burawoy (2005a) has theorized not only sociological labor, but also the labor of public administration scholars. The boundaries that he has constructed not only quadricate intellectual labor within the discipline of sociology, but also distinguish sociological labor from all other forms of academic labor. It seems strange that Burawoy distinguishes "policy sociology" from public administration, except that this distinction protects sociology, albeit artificially, from "collusion" with the state, which would contaminate its standpoint in civil society. Thus, the intellectual functions that public administration performs might be, and often are, the same as those performed by sociologists, but Burawoy does not classify them as sociological. This prevents him from dealing with public administration's own criticisms of the labor performed by "policy sociology." A brief scan of the journal *Administrative Theory and Praxis* would quickly reveal that critical public administration scholars have made extensive arguments against instrumental knowledge boundaries such as Burawoy's. (A comprehensive list would be too exhaustive to include here; for a start, see Box 2005; Box and King 2000; Catlaw 2006; Cunliffe and Jun 2005; Denhardt 1981; Harmon 1995; King and Zanetti 2005; McSwite 1997; Patterson 2001; Schreurs 2003; Stivers 2000a, b; White 1998; Yanow 1996, 2004.)

Although Burawoy (2005a) focuses on retaining policy sociology as "sociology in the service of goal defined by a client" (9), such as the State Department, much of public administration scholarship has moved beyond bureaucracy. As I discuss in Chapter Five, mainstream public administration scholarship has shifted toward governance (see Kettl 2002; Pierre 2000; Rhodes 1996) because divisions of labor and bureaucracy no longer "fit" capitalism's new flexibility requirements (Gantman 2005; Boltanksi and Chiapello 2005). Before it took on the label *governance,* this shift "from government to governance" belonged to a host of neoliberal privatization strategies known as "new public management" (NPM) and the "reinvention of government," which reduced citizen-state interaction to an economic exchange between customer and entrepreneur (Denhardt and Denhardt 2003, 549), while also claiming to reduce the size of government bureaucracies.

This trend of contracting out and privatization led to the *hollow state,* a phrase that began circulating as early as 1993 (Milward, et al. 1993). H. Brinton Milward and Keith G. Provan (2000) indicate that:

> By the hollow state we mean the degree of separation between a government and the services it funds (i.e., the number of layers between the source and the use of funds) ... the hollow state refers to any joint production situation where a governmental agency relies on others (firms, nonprofits, or other government agencies) to jointly deliver public services. Carried to extreme, it refers to a government that as a matter of public policy has chosen to contract out all its production capability to third parties, perhaps retaining only a systems integration function that is responsible for negotiating, monitoring, and evaluating contracts. The central task of the hollow state ... is to arrange networks rather than to carry out the traditional task of government, which is to manage hierarchies. (362)

The phrases "hollow state" and "privatization" evolved into what is now discussed as "governance." For Milward and Provan (2000), "*Governance* is a more inclusive term, concerned with creating the conditions for ordered rule and collective action, often including agents in the private and non-profit sectors as well as within the public sector" (360). The growth of "non" governmental organizations emerges in tandem with the hollowing out of the state and the so-called shift from government to governance, which I discuss in Chapter Five. I discuss the phrases *nonprofit sector* and *nongovernmental organization* (NGO) further in Chapter Four, but in considering the institutionalization of public sociology, it is important to keep in mind that the nonprofit sector and nongovernmental organizations to which it refers are involved in governing.

The Institutionalization of Public Sociology

Knowledge is not only a technique of governing, but is itself governed through those institutions charged with its legitimation. Knowledge does not emerge as true or false, good or bad; it circulates through what Foucault (1980) called an "ensemble of practice." In the case of the social sciences, these ensembles of practice are embedded in disciplinary associations, such as the American Anthropological Association, the American Society of Criminology, the American Political Science Association, or the American Sociological Association. These professional institutions control the circulation of knowledge through accreditation of curricula, annual conferences representing "the state of the field," and the publication and circulation of peer-reviewed journals, such as the *American Anthropologist, American Political Science Review, Criminology,* and *American Sociological Review,* which represent knowledge that has been sanctioned by the discipline.

These regimes of knowledge/power (Foucault 1980) govern the boundaries of the discipline. The question of how public sociology will be treated by the ASA is "a question of what *governs* statements, and the way in which they *govern* each other so as to constitute a set of propositions which are scientifically acceptable.... In short, there is a problem of the regime, the politics of the scientific statement" (Foucault 1980, 112–113). If it was initially celebrated as a critical stance, public sociology was quickly absorbed into this regime. Within two years of his Presidential Address, Burawoy's campaign for public sociology had become widely institutionalized, not only within the publishing and conference circuits, but also within the ASA and a handful of academic programs.

In 2005, the "ASA Task Force on Institutionalizing Public Sociologies" was established to address the question of how public sociology would be incorporated into this regime and transformed into "official" or "legitimate" knowledge (Apple 2003). The task force (2005) report, which employs Burawoy's definition of public sociology (2), details how in "August 2004 the Task Force on Institutionalizing of Public Sociologies was charged with developing proposals for the recognition and validation of public sociology, incentive and rewards for doing public sociology, and evaluating public sociology" (2).

Public sociology thus became an object of governing, subject to standards set by the task force and submitted to the ASA for legitimation. The ASA task force (2007) recognized that public sociology "is the 'public face' of the discipline ... there is a strong need to establish clear standards for evaluating public sociology. In the absence of standards, public sociology is not subject to the routine scrutiny of colleagues and experts in the field" (1). The task force therefore aimed to govern public sociology through the creation of an ensemble of practices. Among the task force's (2005) 17 recommendations are "the mainstreaming of public sociology panels at ASA conferences" (5), an ASA Council review and endorsement of "public sociology tenure and promotion guidelines" (3), and the development of a "public sociology career guide" (4).

The establishment of the ASA task force and the "mainstreaming" of public sociology should not necessarily be interpreted as a movement toward the transformation of the discipline. Guidelines for how to fit public sociology into the discipline as it already exists draw what is potentially a critical stance *against* the institution *into* the institution itself, where it can be disciplined. The "recognition of public sociology" *through the lens of professional sociology* is a means of disciplining the margin: "it is crucial for the discipline to sanitize the names the marginalia give to themselves, ensuring that politics is subordinated to their science and thus taming them" (Agger 1989b, 146). As Glenn (2007) observes of Burawoy's inclusion of public sociology in his division of labor: "from a subaltern perspective, it can also be seen as a way of containing and controlling them. By spelling out what kinds of knowledge each specialized in and what its audiences are, Burawoy's scheme defines 'proper' aims and activities of each wing" (221).

As it became institutionalized, "legitimate public sociology knowledge" gradually conformed to the conflation of "legitimate knowledge" and "job skills." Within five years of Burawoy's Presidential Address, American University had established an MA Concentration in Public Sociology (MAPS), Humboldt State University had established the Public Sociology, Ecological Justice and Action MA program, Saint Louis University had established a Master's Program in Public Sociology, and the University of North Carolina at Wilmington (UNCW) had established a Public Sociology Program. Although these programs build on a tradition known as *applied sociology*—a term coined by the first president of the ASA to describe the instrumentalization of sociological knowledge for bureaucratic purposes (Ward 1906)—in their stated program objectives they are oriented toward training students in what have traditionally been considered public service professions, or "state work" (Harney 2002).

The American University (AU) MAPS "leads to career paths ranging from grassroots organizing and work in community-based non-profit agencies and non-governmental organizations to employment in government agencies, legislative offices, 'think tanks,' advocacy organizations, or private consulting" (American University 2007). The program emphasizes that the faculty is staffed by "sociologists who work in government, community-based non-profits, research, or commercial/consulting organizations" (American University 2007). These staff are representative of Burawoy's policy sociologists, or what Robert K. Merton (1957) categorized as bureaucratic intellectuals, who are decidedly *not* autonomous from the state. At the time of the program's founding, the advisory board for MAPS situated the public sociology program within a broader knowledge regime through the inclusion of: the Director of Education, Workforce and Income Security, U.S. General Accounting Office; the assistant director, Office of International Health, National Institutes of Health; research coordinator, Immigration Statistics Staff Population Division, U.S. Department of Commerce; Minority Professional Staff, United States House of Representatives; and employees from the National Institutes of Health and the U.S. Census Bureau (American University 2007). The inclusion of these government representatives on an advisory board for a public sociology program seriously challenges the realization of Burawoy's call for public sociology to challenge the neoliberal state through the pursuit of reflexive knowledge.

The intersection between the institutionalization of public sociology and governing is further demonstrated in the designation "official public sociology knowledge." The MAPS curriculum includes "projects that involve teamwork, engage decision-makers and community groups, and develop a range of capabilities that can include: needs assessment and strategic planning, managing data collection using a range of methods of observation, interpretation of findings informed by social theory, evaluation of social programs and policies and grant writing" (American University 2007). The public sociology programs at Humboldt State University, Saint Louis University, and UNCW share in common with AU an emphasis on nonprofit organizations and instrumental knowledge. Featured in the ASA newsletter, *Footnotes*, the UNCW program was described as including: "a course focused on doing evaluation research, training in writing for a non-academic audience, interdisciplinary collaboration opportunities, grant-writing workshops, and extended discussion of the differences between academic culture and the cultures of community and not for-profit organizations" (Murphy 2007, 5). Like the AU program, the MA program in public sociology at UNCW is situated within a broader knowledge regime, having been "created in part thanks to funding from the Council of Graduate Schools and the Alfred P. Sloan Foundation" (Murphy 2007, 5). After framing the program according to Burawoy's definition of public sociology (also used to frame the task force and the public sociology program at UNCW), Humboldt State University's (2010) Public Sociology, Ecological Justice and Action MA program "prepares students for professional positions in research, business, government and non-profit organizations" and includes an emphasis in teaching sociology, which "prepares students for community college and other education-related professional positions" (Humboldt State University 2010). Similarly, the MA program in public sociology at Saint Louis University prepares students to "move on to careers as *evaluators, researchers, planners, managers, program directors, and policy makers*" (Saint Louis University 2010).

These four curricular institutionalizations of public sociology blur the boundaries between Burawoy's (2005a, 9) public sociology and policy sociology, thus dissolving the supposed boundary between reflexive and instrumental knowledge. The convergence of public sociology, as it is institutionalized in public sociology curricula, and the instrumental knowledge of the state is found in the curricular overlap with the National Association of Schools of Public Affairs and Administration (NASPAA) curriculum requirements. NASPAA accredits Master of Public Administration (MPA) programs that train students:

In the Management of Public Service Organizations, the components of which include:

- Human resources
- Budgeting and financial processes
- Information management, technology applications, and policy

In the Application of Quantitative and Qualitative Techniques of Analysis, the components of which include:

- Policy and program formulation, implementation, and evaluation
- Decision-making and problem-solving

With an Understanding of the Public Policy and Organizational Environment, the components of which include:

- Political and legal institutions and processes
- Economic and social institutions and processes
- Organization and management concepts and behavior (NASPAA 2008).

Thus we find in common between master's programs in public sociology and the MPA the following:

Skills
- Decision making
- Research methods
- Program formulation/Grant writing
- Evaluation
- Management of organizations and groups
- Governance

Employment Spheres
- The state and its institutions
- The nonprofit sector
- Think tanks

In each instance, the emphasis is on skills constituted by that knowledge that Burawoy (2005a) has classified not as the reflexive knowledge of public sociology, but as the instrumental knowledge employed by professional and policy sociology. Additionally, according to Burawoy's division of sociological labor, these students are trained to be policy sociologists.

Although these appear to be strong academic programs, and there is nothing particularly unusual about training students in applied sociology, it is telling that Burawoy's definition of public sociology is *institutionalized* as applied sociology, or policy sociology: The epistemological practice of public sociology departs from his ontological portrayal. This convergence of public administration and sociology around the practice of governing as instrumental knowledge is explained by Alasdair MacIntyre (1981) as a dual justification for *stabilization,* which requires dual knowledge and expertise: "Government itself becomes a hierarchy of bureaucratic managers, and the major justification advanced for the intervention of government in society is the contention that government has resources of competence which most citizens do not possess.... Expertise becomes a commodity for which rival state agencies and rival private corporations compete. Civil servants and managers alike justify their claims to authority, power and money by invoking their own competence as scientific managers of social change ..." (82). As "expertise becomes a commodity for which rival state agencies and rival private corporations compete," the *production* of expertise becomes a commodity over which knowledge producers compete. It might be the case that public administration now competes with public sociology to produce the expertise over which rival state agencies, nonprofits, and think tanks compete in order to justify their claims to authority, power, and money by invoking skill sets including decision making, research methods, program formulation/grant writing, evaluation, management of organizations and groups, and governance.

Public sociology, institutionalized as the production of expertise according to the demands for instrumental knowledge that can contribute "value" in the form of "better technologies of governing," is characteristic of the demands of "performativity" (Lyotard 1984). Public sociology becomes an "optimal investment strategy" for university departments to the extent that it responds to the imperatives of governing. Public sociology, as it has been institutionalized, can open doors to participation in status networks, as in the case of AU's advisory board, and grant funding, as in the case of UNCW's public sociology program being established "thanks to funding from the Council of Graduate Schools and the Alfred P. Sloan Foundation." Public sociology is situated in a university environment in which "academic managers increasingly view their institution's departments as holdings in a portfolio of assets, rather than as domains of knowledge that society at large and students in particular need to acquire as part of overall educational advancement" (Luke 2005, 19). Through its institutionalization as the production of skill sets that fit the state, the nonprofit sector, and think tanks, public sociology "invokes its competence as a contributor to scientific management of social change" (MacIntyre 1981, 82) and keeps pace with "networks of knowledge production, consumption, circulation, and accumulation," which are embedded in "professional consultancies, for-profit enterprises, and state agencies" (Luke 2005, 26).

Note

1. The reference to the 2005 Address is an error; Burawoy's Address was published in 2005, but was the 2004 Presidential Address.

Chapter 3

Public Sociology as Knowledge, Politics, and Portrayal

Since Burawoy's 2004 campaign, to say that one is an advocate of public sociology no longer necessarily conveys a critical stance toward the current practice of professional sociology. It has become difficult for those who advocate public sociology in the critical tradition of C. Wright Mills even to discuss public sociology without becoming bogged down in assumptions with which they do not agree, including Burawoy's (2005a) explicit rejection of the possibility of Mills's sociological imagination (9). Given the dominance of Burawoy's portrayal, evidenced by its institutionalization in the ASA and public sociology curricula, to speak on behalf of public sociology might now imply that one agrees with the idea of an organic division of labor and that one agrees that sociological knowledge can be categorized according to two audiences (academic and extra-academic) and two epistemologies (instrumental and reflexive). This raises concerns about the way in which representations of our experience in the world, such as organic divisions of labor, and incorrect assumptions about the neutrality of knowing, such as the positivism and instrumental knowledge produced by professional sociology, invisibly govern everyday knowledge about the possibility for transformation.

Although there has been extensive discussion of Burawoy's portrayal of public sociology as deriving from an organic division of labor rooted in professional sociology, this limited focus on Burawoy's recent campaign as the focal point of public sociology neglects the historic contestability of the politics of sociological knowledge and intellectual activity more broadly considered. In this chapter I critically consider Agger's and Burawoy's competing conceptions of sociological labor and their implications for the production of knowledge. I use the contrast between Agger's (2000) and Burawoy's (2005a) recent calls for public sociology as a lens through which to understand the ways in which the narratives produced by sociological labor govern the emergence of knowledge that would be a basis of transformation.[1] I argue that Burawoy's organic division of labor is an ontological fiction stabilized by epistemological boundaries, which in turn, disguise the relationship between sociological knowledge and the neoliberal state, thus forestalling transformation. I conclude that Burawoy's public sociology is derived from the same assumptions that have produced the problems he argues public sociology ought to oppose.

Burawoy's Ontological Fiction

Public intellectuality is not a new idea, a fact that both Agger and Burawoy recognize; however, the history of public intellectuality has been rewritten by Burawoy as belonging to an organic evolution toward his taken-for-granted division of labor. As I explained in the Introduction, thinkers at least since Marx have criticized the idea of professionalized knowledge, with the hope that, through recognition that *intellectuals govern through the creation of knowledge about possibility,* a sphere of discourse aimed at improving the world might be achieved. Agger's (2000) conception of public sociology belongs to this critical tradition. Public sociology for Agger is *transformative*; it is positioned in opposition to professional sociology's tendency to deny that it is authored by individuals with political sensibilities and thus to invisibly order the social world, resulting in a decline of discourse (see Agger 1989a, 1989b, 1989c, 1990, 1991b, 1992a). For Agger (2000), *public sociology* was a phrase used to advocate the transformation of sociological labor in such a way that writers would anticipate and value readers' criticisms and be open to the public's revision of sociological ideas, thereby inviting public debate. Agger's (2000) argument, as the subtitle of his book indicates, was that professional sociology did not mirror inalterable social facts, but was always a literary practice that constituted a political stance. Agger does not call, as Burawoy does, for a division of labor that distinguishes public from critical from professional from policy sociology; Agger's call is for professional sociology to become public sociology through a transformation of hierarchies of labor established through knowledge production in order to reverse the decline of public discourse (see Agger 1990).

Although both Agger and Burawoy argue on behalf of sociological practice that addresses major social problems, this is the only clear similarity between their usages of the phrase *public sociology.* Curiously, Burawoy has styled his argument as a Marxist stance: He uses eleven theses after Marx's *Theses on Feuerbach*; he titled his ASA Presidential Address "For Public Sociology" (2005a) after Louis Althusser's 1965 "For Marx"; and he titled a later public sociology piece "What Is To Be Done? Theses on the Degradation of Social Existence in a Globalizing World" (2008) after Vladimir Lenin's famous 1901 essay, "What Is To Be Done?" which addressed the role of intellectuals in revolution. Yet, in his Presidential Address Burawoy used the phrase *public sociology* to describe something entirely different from Marx's initial critical stance and Agger's 2000 conception. As Paul Paolucci (2008, 382) has argued of Burawoy's mainstream public sociology program, "with its conflation of scientific discourse with political action, and its pronouncements on abstract principles such as democracy, freedom, and justice, public sociology is neither Marxist nor radical." Burawoy's (2005a) eleven theses "for public sociology," unlike Marx's theses or Agger's critical public sociology, are *not* aimed at transformation of the intellectual endeavor known as sociology; Burawoy (2005a) very clearly indicates that his definition of public sociology is an addition to the field as he claims that it already exists. Indeed, as I discussed in Chapter Two, Burawoy's (2005c) argument is positioned *against* the radicalization of sociology: "Let me be clear, our disciplinary project cannot and should not be reduced to *critical sociology*, which makes no sense without a *professional sociology* to criticize or even without a *public sociology* to infuse with its commitments, just as all three find their complement in a *policy sociology* with its more instrumental deployment of knowledge" (318).

My reading of Burawoy's text is that it is not primarily a call for public sociology, but is instead primarily an argument for the legitimacy of professional sociology and instrumental knowledge employed by the state. Burawoy (2005a) frames public sociology as belonging to an "organic" division of labor. Note well that Burawoy's use of the word *organic* in relation to labor is far more Durkheimian than Gramscian. Given that an "organic division of labor for sociology" is the basis of Burawoy's 2004 argument for public sociology, it is worth noting that in 1893 when Emile Durkheim originally wrote of the division of labor (specialization), he argued that it emerged not as a matter of choice, but as a matter of social law to which human choice is irrelevant. The division of labor, Durkheim argued, is necessary to maintain solidarity, or *order*. In other words, it is a necessary formation for the continuation of legitimate governing.

Burawoy's call for public sociology is much more than a call for *public* sociology. Public sociology seems an afterthought for Burawoy when one considers that this division of labor is a statement on behalf of:

- ending discussion about the transformation of professional sociology
- bureaucratic intellectuals (Merton 1957) producing instrumental knowledge

- critical sociologists sequestered from the public
- the uselessness of reflexive knowledge for public policy
- the illegitimacy of the public's reflexive knowledge about the policy that governs their lives

Public sociology, according to Burawoy's (2005a) fictional account of what exists within the discipline of sociology, is an argument for professional sociology and instrumental knowledge: "there can be neither policy nor public sociology without a *professional sociology* that supplies true and tested methods, accumulated bodies of knowledge, orienting questions, and conceptual frameworks" (10). Again, this is *not* an argument for public sociology; it is an argument for professional sociology. Public sociology is framed by Burawoy (2005a) as *a source of legitimacy* for professional sociology and professional sociology is said to be "the *sine qua non* of public sociology's existence" (10). Indeed, Burawoy (2005a) also argues that critical sociology is dependent on professional sociology: "Without a professional sociology, there can be no policy or public sociology, but nor can there be a critical sociology—for there would be nothing to criticize" (15). *All* sociological labor is written by Burawoy to be dependent on the reification of professional sociology, just as neoliberalism is dependent on the state's reification of instrumental knowledge to the exclusion of transformative knowledges. This division of labor smacks of Piccone's (1978) artificial negativity. For Piccone, it would be impossible for public sociology to emerge within a division of labor that legitimates artificial negativity based on the primacy of that which it opposes.

In arguing that Burawoy has generated an ontological fiction, I am arguing that he has generated a myth of an organic division of sociological labor in order to stabilize a world that simply does not exist, namely, a world in which professional sociology's instrumental knowledge does not govern possibility. The boundaries between Burawoy's (2005a) role categories for sociologists give the false illusion that positivist and instrumental professional sociology and policy sociology do not *result* in a disengaged and discouraged public, thus preventing the successful emergence of reflexive critical sociology and public sociology. For Agger (2000), this emergence is dependent on the realization that U.S. professional sociology and policy sociology are literary acts, open for revision, not professionalized facts, which people fail to recognize as being political and thus changeable. It is for this reason that Agger (1989c) rejects the idea that professional sociology based in seemingly authorless science can coexist with public sociology: Positivist and instrumental professionalism are destructive in relationship to public life because the public falsely internalizes "facts" and utility as inalterable truths (Agger 1989a, 1989b, 1989c, 2000). This was Agger's (2007) point when, in his conceptualization of public sociology, he wrote that "a public sociology must want to change the world, and it *must recognize that it is already changing the world by intervening in it*" (270, my emphasis). When Burawoy (2004a) wrote that public sociology promotes "dialogue about issues that affect the fate of society" (104) he failed to recognize that it is also the practice of professional sociology, which he endorses, that affects the fate of society as it "secretly writes" the world (Agger 1989c, 2000).

It is closer to the truth than is Burawoy's division of labor that when intellectuals produce professional sociology that fails to reveal that it is a political stance (Agger 1989c, 2000), the public response is a decline in discourse, because discourse depends on the assumption that *knowledge, including expert knowledge, is political* (Agger 1990, 33–34). Burawoy (2004b) has rejected Agger's earlier conception of public sociology except to say that "Ben Agger's *Public Sociology* is a minute analysis of the pathologies of professional sociology, but says curiously little about public sociology and *its* dilemmas" (126). Yet, read through Agger's lens, Burawoy's (2005a) insistence that public sociology is dependent on professional sociology neglects that professional sociology exercises authority over the public sphere with consequences for the possibility of public sociology.

Agger's (2000) core argument in his conception of public sociology is that when professional sociology's positivist science dominates intellectual production it also dominates a public that, in response, fails to read science as resulting from questions that are themselves political. Thus, for Agger (1990), a reifying division of sociological labor such as Burawoy's (2005a) would be in part responsible for the decline in public discourse. This is so because when professional sociology produces the world as "social facts" rather than as a literary acts, it is exclusionary by virtue of secretly claiming authorial authority over the social world, where such authority could otherwise be claimed by a public that realized that *they too could intervene in the world* (Agger 1989a, 1989b, 1989c, 1990, 1991b, 2000). The loss of the category *alterable* through the declaration of professional boundaries eclipses the possibility of the public participating in the narration of their social world and thus eclipses the possibility of public sociology. Professional sociology in this way is distinctly anti-discursive in that it excludes the possibility of change and in doing so excludes the public.

The current practice of professional sociology reified in Burawoy's table not only contributes to the decline of public discourse, it also contributes to the decline of public sociologists. Burawoy's (2004a, 2004b, 2004c, 2004d, 2005a, 2005b) claim to a division of labor for sociology reifies an *unnecessary* hierarchy of value imposed according to academia's reliance on literary political economy,[2] which mirrors the neoliberal state's reliance on the market (Harvey 2007). It is empirically untrue that appearing in public, even appearing intelligent, is the standard for determination of the value of one's academic labor, which is solely determined by the ranking of the academic journals in which one's writing appears: "The commodification of academic writing structures quite differential career outcomes. Some people's work is 'less' worthy than that of others simply *by virtue of where it appeared, not what it says*" (Agger 1990, 136). Academic survival is determined not by the size of one's audience, but by a hierarchy of literary value. Luke (1999) explains that:

> the placement of articles and books become the blue book of one's career or the means for assaying the placement of one's labor in departments, between different universities, or within the discipline itself. Without any other stable measure of value, the systems of continuous normalizing judgment typically use obvious indicators of status, like institutional location or professional position to measure worth.... "Where" one publishes and "how often," then, clearly are accepted as a definition of "worth" for ranking in these networks of production. (349–350)

The choice to engage in public or critical sociology instead of professional or policy sociology has to be situated in these relations of value. As Arlene Stein (2009) notes, "hierarchies of prestige and power are inherent in the rankings of academic journals and graduate departments.... Particularly when competition for employment and promotion is fierce, greater rewards accrue to those who adopt professional identities that conform closely to hegemonic understandings of the discipline" (161). Given these built-in enforcement mechanisms, Burawoy's (2004a, 105) reminder to professional sociology that it must "discipline" critical sociology might not be necessary at all!

An "organic" division of labor such as Burawoy's (2004a, b, c, d, 2005a, b), like a sexual division of labor, "conceals hierarchy underneath nature-like differentiation" (Agger 1993, 142).[3] In Agger's (1993, 142) feminist conception, the logic of the division of labor is a hierarchical division, allowing for the valued to dominate the valueless. Burawoy's division of labor, which *differentiates* theory and *specifies* instrumental knowledge, is addressed by Agger in 1991b: "We must challenge the positivist definition of scholarly legitimacy—surveys, computers, grants, value-freedom—and instead insist on the validity of non-instrumental, non-quantitative knowledge. We must argue that theory *matters,* even if it defies easy domestication in the prevailing academic division of labor, which sets up rigid boundaries among specialties" (103). This is a key point in response to Burawoy's (2004a, b, c, d, 2005a, b) tacit statement that all sociological labor is equally valued; in truth, legitimated labor is valued more in sociology because the "open market of ideas," like the free markets that Burawoy (2008) is critical of, is an illusion (Agger 1991b, 103).

The institutions in which sociologists are employed value that which stabilizes the present over that which would require radical transformation (Nickel 2008). Sociological labor, like all other labor in a capitalist state, is produced within the realm of valued and valueless activity (Agger 1989a, 60–61). This circuitry is as relevant to Burawoy's division of labor as it is to household divisions of labor. The discipline of sociology assigns value according to which authors it is willing to employ and what authorship it is willing to publish. Public sociology cannot be transformative for any public unless it is also transformative for sociologists. If sociology is truly to go public, it must assign *value* to critical public sociology as something other than pro-professional sociological labor. We can easily rearrange Burawoy's (2005a) boxes to reflect how sociological labor typically functions in the day-to-day management of a junior scholar's career in North America:

Table 3-1 Sociology's "Actually Existing" Division of Labor

	Valued	*Valueless*
Functional	PROFESSIONAL POLICY DISCOURSE	
Transformative		CRITICAL PUBLIC INTELLECTUALITY

Neglect of the relations of value in Table 3-1 is damaging not only for the public, but for the sociologists who are charged with stabilizing Burawoy's ontological fiction. The top row of Burawoy's table (Table 1-1) has more value in the academic marketplace than the bottom row does. This is so because that which is endorsed by one's peers has more value in the discipline of sociology than that which is endorsed by the public. Burawoy (2004a, 105) assigns critical sociology a role as the "conscience of professional sociology." The "role" of the conscience of professional sociology is a secondary and servile one: Professional sociology still *dominates,* especially given that Burawoy (2004a) has assigned professional sociology the role of *disciplining* critical sociology. (See Dahms 2008.) Yet, as Richard Ericson (2005) states: "Sociologists who do work what Burawoy labels critical—for example, feminism, queer theory and critical race theory—are as rigorously professional in their theories and methods as any others! Furthermore, being critical is a core element of professionalism" (366).

Sociology as it is written by Burawoy no longer explains even the lives of sociologists, which are lived in the nexus of the ontological fiction he has created and the resultant myth that our own lives, careers, and voices exist in the supposed "ivory tower" (Burawoy 2008, 358). As far as I know, sociologists buy their milk in "the real world," and they also attempt to find and keep jobs in a world where it is prohibitively difficult for most people to be critical public theorists and also employed in the production of instrumental policy knowledge. The reason that there are few, if any, *critical* sociologists employed as junior scholars in the field of public policy, or even in sociology, in the United States is that knowledge is political, and thus critical knowledge is declared politically illegitimate by those who resist change.

It is naive for Burawoy (2004a) to write that "graduate students may start out as critical sociologists, become professional sociologists, and then later turn to public sociology" (106). In today's job market, which is dominated by professional sociology, most graduate students are told that they must start out as professional sociologists and that only when tenured may they turn to critical and public sociology. Jonathan Imber (2001) specifically cautions against Agger's (2000) advice that graduate students carve out a career as critical public sociologists: "Agger tries to imagine a world made safe for poetic sociology, even one that speaks of justice to the masses.... In the meantime, his hope for public sociology is potentially perilous advice for those risking a career in academic sociology. If you are lucky to have Ben Agger guiding (or Stanley Fish as a second letter), you might get promoted (or at least hired). The real lament is that so many of the unguided get stuck in what Alfred Whitehead rightly called the groove. And this is *after* tenure" (354).

Although Imber was writing three years before Burawoy's (2004a) mainstream endorsement of public sociology, Burawoy's assumption that one can easily traverse the division of labor in sociology is specious. Junior scholars and future public sociologists cannot choose both the bottom row and the top row of Burawoy's (2004a) division of labor, because the top row stabilizes the discipline (and thus the world) as it is, while the bottom row is aimed at transformation. Burawoy might reply that he has retained a space for critical public sociologists, but when the academy chooses to employ knowledge producers, they usually employ those whose stance is legitimated and legitimating and thus employ the top row.

The legitimacy of one's knowledge claims is already dictated by one's possession of "positional goods" and status indicators, including institutional location and professional position (Luke 1999, 350). These positional goods are governed by what Luke (1999) identifies as "ranking regimes," which operate according to deeply embedded systems of sign-value, which in turn structure academic careers (350–351). For example, a sociologist submits an article to the ASA-appointed editor of *American Sociological Review*. The editor will decide whether the article is immediately rejected or sent out for blind peer review. When the sociologist submits the article, he or she will include a cover letter printed on university letterhead or attach it to an e-mail sent from a university address. In spite of the fact that one's institutional affiliation provides no guarantee of the quality of one's work, it is assumed by at least some authors that the higher the ranking of the university named on their letterhead or e-mail address, the more likely it is that their article will be reviewed. I know academics who have rushed to submit articles before finishing their PhD programs, because they wanted to take advantage of the university's letterhead before they moved to their job at a lower-ranked university. They considered the highly ranked university's letterhead to be more advantageous than either their PhD or the quality of their work. This is what Alvin Gouldner (1970) discussed as the "treatment of [an intellectual's] *work* in its *intellectual* market" (200). Sociology thus comes to be legitimated and valued not by what the author conveys, but by the "positional goods" (Luke 1999) that one possesses at the time of submission, including institutional affiliation with highly ranked universities that are valued as status symbols for the journal. One reason that it is assumed that editors might be influenced by an author's letterhead is that they are responsible for maintaining the journal's ranking, which is at least informally influenced by the ranking of the universities where published authors are positioned.

It is not enough in today's academic marketplace to have one's work sanctioned in some public space; it must be sanctioned by organizations and journals that reject most work, such as *American Sociological Review*, which in 2009 had an acceptance rate of 7 percent. Public intellectuality in the sense of circulating one's work for public debate in highly circulated but lowly ranked spaces has little value in the economy of the academic career, which is why the ASA task force was concerned with tenure and promotion guidelines: What would it mean for the authority of the discipline if public sociology, rather than professional sociology, was the standard for tenure and promotion? Consider Judith Stacey's (2007) suggestions for the radicalization of the discipline toward the emergence of a transformative public sociology:

> Declare a moratorium on academic publishing by all full-time faculty members in each department. At staggered intervals of perhaps one year out of every three, departmental faculty would be precluded from submitting any work for publication in a peer-reviewed journal or press.... Abolish the rank of associate professor.... Expand the charge of the new ASA task force for public sociology, or perhaps establish a broader commission, to develop model disciplinary guidelines for promotion ... that directly counter assembly-line standards of productivity.... (96–97)

Stacey's suggestions reveal in contrast how conservative Burawoy's division of labor is in relationship to the academic career.

Transformative public sociology stands little chance of emerging from within a fictional division of labor that stabilizes the instrumental rationality of professional sociology. Professional sociology, like policy sociology, is based in the illegitimacy of particular forms of knowledge, specifically those that do not fall within the disciplines' existing boundaries. Burawoy's institutionalization of knowledge and intellectuals thus involves political choice—what counts as knowledge is politically determined and, in the case of a reifying division of sociological labor, what counts as legitimate sociology is politically determined. As Michael Apple (2003) explains, knowledge boundaries act as a source of legitimacy for official knowledge (11). The pro-professional public sociology that Burawoy has constructed is based in concrete knowledge boundaries. It is through such exclusions, particularly the official exclusion of knowledge, that power functions. "Out of the vast universe of possible knowledge, only some knowledge and ways of knowing it get declared to be legitimate or 'official.' … Official knowledge is the result of conflicts and compromises both within the state and between the state and civil society" (Apple 2003, 7). It is only through the declaration of public and critical sociology as *unprofessional* sociology that professional sociology can be maintained. Sociology's professionalism is constituted through a self-determined boundary of legitimacy, as Burawoy (2005a) declared when he wrote that "there can be neither policy nor public sociology without a *professional sociology*" (10). What Burawoy (2005a) has done is constitute the legitimacy of professional sociology through the determination of all other sociologies as somehow less legitimate by virtue of *not* being professional sociology.

From Fiction to Function

Attempts such as Burawoy's to stabilize triumphant disciplines as "public" do little to generate critical public intellectuality and discourse, which would not be particularly concerned with the academy's legitimacy or even necessarily recognize disciplines and their professional governing codes of practice as legitimate at all. Rather than creating the professional and economic conditions necessary for public intellectuals to thrive, these pro-disciplinary campaigns for public intellectuals might instead serve as legitimating narratives on behalf of the disciplinary dominance that resulted in the decline of public intellectuals in the first place. As Foucault (1995, 2002) recognized, discipline is practiced exactly through binaries such as professional/unprofessional.

Like all dichotomies, Burawoy's boxes tell only half of the story. If one reads between the lines, Burawoy has constructed a hierarchy in which critical sociology cannot be professional sociology, public sociology cannot be critical sociology, and policy sociology cannot be public sociology. Unpacked, Burawoy's boxes spill forth two more false assumptions: that there is a clean boundary between an academic audience and an extra-academic audience and that there is a *necessary* boundary between the profession, criticism, reflexivity, and practice. The false assumption of clean boundaries[4] stems from Burawoy's failure to recognize that the world is already influenced by positivism and instrumental knowledge. This was Agger's (1989b) point when he argued that socio(onto)logy is "world-constitutive" (304). Where professional sociology creates a positivist culture (Agger 1989a), the extra-academic audience is *already constituted* by the academic audience. Burawoy incorrectly assumes that only knowledge that is *intended* for an extra-academic audience influences the extra-academic world. When Burawoy (2004c) writes that "*public sociology engages publics beyond the academy in dialogue about matters of political and* moral concern" (1607), he fails to recognize that political and moral concerns are already determined by a public sphere that gives more value to instrumental knowledge than to reflexive knowledge. According to this assumption, policy intellectuals are not critical or reflexive, critical and public intellectuals are not policy intellectuals, and policy and the public are divorced.

The false assumption of a *necessary* boundary between profession, criticism, and reflexivity assumes that professional sociology is not already political. Knowledge and practice are political for professional and policy sociology, just as they are for critical and public sociology. Read outside of their neatly packed boxes, Burawoy's sociological laborers fall into the following four categories:

- the unreflexive and unprofessional policy intellectual producing instrumental knowledge for an extra-academic audience
- the unreflexive professional intellectual producing knowledge for an academic audience
- the nonpublic critical intellectual producing reflexive knowledge for an academic audience
- the unprofessional public intellectual producing reflexive knowledge for an extra-academic audience

Public sociology needs to start with an understanding of how professional and policy sociology are *valued* in relationship to critical and public sociology and thus how power is hierarchically distributed within the field. I take from Agger that Burawoy is overly optimistic to think that most sociologists will dedicate their careers to "public labor," as long as he subjugates public and critical labor to "professional" and "policy" labor. No one does public sociology for tenure. Those who do public sociology do it for the public and often at cost to their "professional" career. As Derber (2004) rightly points out: "Burawoy's assumption of an essential complementarity among the four sociologies masks deep tensions among them" (119). This is precisely so because public sociology, according to Burawoy (2004a, b, c, d, 2005a, b), is *not professional sociology* and thus does not "count" for advancement within the profession.

Pro-Professional Public Sociology's Contribution to Neoliberalism

The possibility of public sociology emerging from sociology's actually existing division of labor is only one part of the ontological fiction that Burawoy has constructed. The third phase of Burawoy's (2008) campaign for pro-professional public sociology is an argument for a sociology positioned against "third-wave marketization"[5] in concert with civil society, by which sociology "lives and dies" (354). This stance against neoliberalism, though laudable, cannot emerge from Burawoy's ontological fiction, which stabilizes instrumental knowledge. If it is true that sociology lives and dies by civil society, it is also true that neoliberalism practiced by the capitalist state lives and dies by the instrumental knowledge that Burawoy defends. Embedded within Burawoy's (2005a) division of labor are an instrumental theory of knowledge (professional and policy sociology), an affirmative theory of the liberal capitalist state (policy sociology), and several incompatible theories of intellectual labor; however, the relationship between knowledge, the neoliberal state, and intellectual labor and their amalgamated influence on public life seems to be unproblematic for Burawoy. This is to say, public life is governed by instrumental knowledge produced by intellectuals in relationship with the neoliberal state, but Burawoy disguises this relationship through the creation of governing boundaries that are based in affirmation of the very instrumental knowledge that sustains the problems that he claims to oppose.

This is important because, given that Burawoy's call for public sociology is in fact a call for the legitimacy of professional sociology, it is not possible for us to consider his argument for public sociology independent of the ways in which professional and policy sociology—instrumental knowledge—govern through what Timothy Mitchell (2002) calls techno-politics and "rule by experts." Although Burawoy has separated professional and policy sociology in terms of their audience, he has maintained that they share a legitimate instrumental orientation toward public life. It is therefore necessary for us to consider the relationship between instrumental knowledge, which Burawoy supports, and the neoliberal state, which Burawoy claims to oppose. Instrumental knowledge stabilizes the logic of productivity that rules the market, the state, and the academic career. Neoliberalism, what Burawoy has called "third-wave marketization," is sustained exactly by instrumental knowledge as the basis for the "necessity" of productivity.

My argument that instrumental knowledge governs possibility on behalf of the market builds on the Frankfurt School's critique of instrumental knowledge as an instrument of domination. Burawoy's attempt to achieve liberation from the market through the stabilization of instrumental rationality is untenable. As Max Horkheimer (1974) argued in the *Eclipse of Reason,* "reason has become an instrument ... completely harnessed to the social process. Its operational value, its role in the domination of men and nature, has been made the sole criterion" (21). Burawoy does not seem to understand that the domination of nature and the neoliberal state stem from the same thing: the instrumental knowledge that he defends, not once, but at least seven times (2004a, 2004b, 2004c, 2004d, 2005a, 2005b, 2005c). That Burawoy (2007c, 2008) bases the second phase of his campaign in Karl Polanyi's *The Great Transformation* is misleading, given that Polanyi

(1944) himself viewed instrumental rationality employed as an industrial revolution to be a "catastrophe" (41). Burawoy's (2008) further criticism of the commodification of nature is similarly oblivious to the fact that, as Horkheimer and Adorno (1989) wrote, domination of nature is the outcome of instrumental knowledge, or enlightenment rationality, which results in totally administered society.

The moral stance that Burawoy asks for public sociologists to take against the market is incompatible with instrumental rationality, which requires all noninstrumental rationality to be "secondary, minor, or exceptional" (Mitchell 2002, 300). In his study of the development rationality that now dominates global politics, Mitchell (2002) finds that the "the binarisms fixed in place in modern politics open up the distance that requires and enables [expertise] … the place and claims of expertise are constituted in the separation that seems to open up, opposing nature to technology, reality to its representation, objects to their value …" (15). A binary is precisely what Burawoy has achieved in his division of labor for sociology: a division that allows for a separation between public sociology's moral stance and professional sociology's instrumental knowledge. As Gouldner (1970) argued of instrumental rationality, it requires "men to be moral cretins in their technical roles … choosing to ignore or to value other meanings and consequences of theories … in effect refusing to take responsibility for them even if they do exist.… The social function of such segmented role structure … is to sever the normal moral sensibilities" (13).

Although Burawoy claims to oppose the market (2007c) and neoliberalism (2008), the neoliberal state is fortified by his division of labor, which protects the validity of the instrumental knowledge upon which the neoliberal state is dependent for its emphasis on productivity, which is exactly the rationale used to support the shift from "welfare to workfare." As the welfare state was on the rise, Gouldner (1970) identified the relationship between sociology and the welfare state as one of mutual fortification. As the welfare state is dismantled, we are witnessing a deepening of this mutual fortification of sociology and the state's approach to well-being in Burawoy's ontological fiction, which, through the instrumentality of knowledge, absolves policy sociologists of responsibility for moral sensibility, now solely the responsibility of pro-professional public sociology.

Professional sociology is not autonomous from neoliberalism. In failing to recognize the politics of knowledge and its moral consequences, Burawoy fails to recognize that the very marketization of which he is critical is possible only through a particular orientation toward knowledge as it is produced by professional sociology, which he is *unwilling to criticize.* Critical theory at least since the Frankfurt School has recognized the relationship between instrumental knowledge, the state, and the market. Neoliberalism silences moral stances, such as those advocated by Burawoy, through the assertion of the primacy of instrumental rationality, which is also advocated by Burawoy. Yet, Burawoy has asked us to base our moral stance against neoliberalism in the primacy of professional sociology and its associated instrumental rationality.

Transformative public sociology is not possible without insisting on the probability that professional sociology's emphasis on instrumental knowledge is contributing to the very problems that public sociology claims to want to end. A public sociology that argues on behalf of the possibility of transformation is possible, but it will not emerge from the ontological fiction that Burawoy has constructed, because it is precisely through such fictions that the neoliberal state functions in concert with instrumental intellectual labor to govern public imagination. As Horkheimer and Adorno (1989) argued: "It is characteristic of the sickness that even the best-intentioned reformer who uses an impoverished and debased language to recommend renewal, by his insidious mode of categorization and the bad philosophy it conceals, strengthens the very power of the established order he is trying to break. False clarity is only another name for myth; and myth has always been obscure and enlightening at one and the same time ..." (xiv).

Critical knowledge cannot be transformative if is portrayed as just another incidental by-product of an "organic" division of labor. A division of labor for sociology that stabilizes the production and employment of instrumental knowledge by professional and policy sociologists is not an argument on behalf of public sociology; it is an argument on behalf of the neoliberal rationale for legitimate governing. Public sociology must first acknowledge the *possibility* for sociologists dominated by professional sociology to stand apart from instrumental knowledge and its employment by the state apparatus, demonstrating to people that it is *possible* to legitimate the knowledge gleaned from their own lived experiences in the world, which are increasingly out of sync with sociology's professional explanations.

Notes

1. The current disagreement between Agger and Burawoy is also reflected in their 1989 debate over the politics of knowledge and the "crisis of Marxism," published in the *Berkeley Journal of Sociology* (Agger 1989d, Burawoy 1989).

2. Burawoy (2008) recently acknowledged this point (359). However, he has offered no explanation of the implications for his division of labor.

3. See Glenn 2007 for an outstanding feminist discussion of how Burawoy's division of labor through logics of exclusion cements hierarchy and marginalization.

4. Although his overall argument is not necessarily compatible with my own, Orlando Patterson (2007) rightly points out that Burawoy constructs "falsely crisp sets and categories" (176).

5. Burawoy uses *third-wave marketization* and *neoliberalism* interchangeably. He first makes this argument as "public sociology vs. the market" in 2007.

Part II

The Expansion of Governing

that their real earnest
has been to grant excuses
for ritual actions

—W. H. Auden, Archaeology, *1973*

Chapter 4

Civil Society and the Origins of the Expansion of Governing

Lately, whatever the problem is, the answer seems to be "more civil society" and less "government." In 1999 Colin Ball and Barry Knight declared that "the world is a mess" and "the cavalry is civil society … which can rescue us from war and from unfettered global capitalism" (19). In 2003 Mary Kaldor titled her discourse on civil society *Global Civil Society: An Answer to War.* In 2002 Anthony Giddens argued that: "The fostering of an active civil society is a basic part of the politics of the third way.… State and civil society should act in partnership, each to facilitate, but also act as a control upon, the other" (78–79). In his call for public sociology, Burawoy (2005c) argued that "critical sociologists should focus less on radicalizing professional sociology, although there is *always* room for that, and more on fostering public sociologies to bolster the organs of civil society" (319). The ubiquity of this "consensual concept" (Chandhoke 2003, 8) makes it difficult to discern exactly what it is that we advocate when we advocate the performance of politics in civil society. The difficulty, according to Michael W. Foley and Bob Edwards (1996), is that "the concept seems to take on the property of gas, expanding or contracting to fit the analytic space afforded it by each historical or sociopolitical setting" (42).

Giddens's portrayal of civil society represents the problem well; civil society seems to be employed to meet whatever the requirements of governing happen to demand of it at a particular point in time: There are "no permanent boundaries between government and civil society … government needs sometimes to be drawn further into the civil arena, sometimes to retreat" (79–80). Giddens's "third way" is one of many phrases to emerge in the past decade to describe governing through civil society: associational democracy (Baccaro 2006; Cohen and Rogers 1995; Warren 2000), collaborative governance (Ansell and Gash 2008; Donahue 2004; Newman, et al., 2004; Sirianni 2009; Zadek 2008), and network governance (Blomgren Bingham, et al. 2005; Sørensen and Torfing 2005a,b) all place an emphasis on fostering relationships between civil society, the state, and, in some cases, the market as the basis for legitimate governing. The subtext of these varying positions on the formation of governing is that civil society is more democratic than the state.

Civil society, like public sociology and governance, lately seems to have acquired an aura of democratic legitimacy. Yet, like public sociology and governance, civil society is a contestable phrase representing a wide variety of ideas and practices. If we are to consider the democratic potentials of civil society, we would first need to know what this ideal represents, as well as what it disguises and legitimates. In order to understand the concept of civil society in relationship to governing, in this chapter I begin by positioning the contemporary emphasis on civil society in historical context. I then explore the relationship between knowledge and governing in order to trace how the ideal of civil society became institutionalized as NGO research. Finally, I question what Burawoy's (2005a) "public sociology from the standpoint of civil society" might entail in relation to governing.

"The Answer Is Civil Society"

Contrary to Burawoy's assertion, civil society is not the exclusive standpoint of sociology. The history of thought about civil society is also the history of thought about how human beings can, do, and should live together. John Ehrenberg (1999) traces the concept of civil society from its classical heritage in ancient Greece through to the contemporary period, demonstrating that the phrase cannot be said to have a stable or absolute meaning, but rather must be understood in historical context. Prior to the contemporary emphasis on governance, the modern notion of civil society could be said to rely on the liberal distinction between the state—national governments that managed national problems—and civil society—a space where citizens of nations engaged in debate about matters of national importance.

Globalization and the emergence of international governance organizations (IGOs) such as the United Nations, the World Bank, and the International Monetary Fund have challenged this liberal nation-based distinction between the state and civil society. In order to portray these supragovernmental organizations as legitimate democratic actors, contemporary cosmopolitan globalization theorists, who claim to depart from liberal theories of the state, have idealized *global* civil society as a space where global public opinion is formed (Beck 2005a; Castells 2008; Kaldor 2003). At whatever level it is conceptualized—national or global—governance in partnership with civil society, which places an emphasis on government by nongovernmental organizations, dilutes what liberal theorists understood as a boundary between the state and civil society.

The contemporary emphasis on civil society as an answer to varying crises of governing emerged during a visibly transformative period, including spectacular images of successful resistance to the government of the Soviet Union by a labor union in Poland in the 1980s, known in the West as the Solidarity movement (see Arato 1981), the global broadcast of images of the dismantling of the Berlin Wall in Germany in 1989, and the end of the Soviet Union in 1991. It seemed to many as though citizen politics practiced in civil society were transforming nation-states. Yet, as Ronaldo Munck (2010) notes, "as the 1990s wore on, [civil society] became less a mode of contesting state power and more a way in which the populations (especially in developing countries) could be incorporated into the anti-statist agenda of the new neoliberal development economics" (318).

Although the radical shift in the relationship between government and labor in the Soviet Union during the 1980s and 1990s was framed as a civil society movement, there were similarly radical shifts in government-labor-market relations during this period that were not celebrated as civil society movements. With the election of President Ronald Reagan in the United States and Prime Minister Margaret Thatcher in Britain, the philosophy of neoliberalism took institutional form through a series of widespread government reforms aimed at weakening labor unions—the same types of organizations that were characterized as radically democratic civil society organizations in Poland.

The emergence of neoliberalism in tandem with a renewed emphasis on civil society helped to set the stage for the framing of civil society in market terms. As a governing strategy, neoliberalism relies on widespread internalization of the givenness of the market as the best possible means to achieve human well-being. In contrast to social rights guaranteed by the welfare state, David Harvey (2007) explains that neoliberalism is "in the first instance a theory of political economic practices that proposes that human well-being can best be achieved by liberating individual entrepreneurial freedoms and private property rights, free markets, and free trade. The role of the state is to create and preserve an institutional framework appropriate to such practices" (2).

Harvey (2007) demonstrates how advocates of neoliberalism frame the ideals of "freedom" and "human dignity" as being dependent on free markets and free trade (7). This is a critical point: Neoliberalism framed limitations on the market as limitations on human well-being and thus closed off the conceptual space necessary to engage in discussion of how the market damages human well-being. Much like the ideal of civil society, the ideals of freedom and human dignity are diluted into what Nancy Fraser (1989) called "thin" interpretations of well-being (163–164). Neoliberalism reduces questions of freedom and human dignity to the market, avoiding the "thicker" questions of what these ideals are in practice and how the market will provide for them. As Harvey (2007) notes: "the assumption that individual freedoms are guaranteed by freedom of the market and of trade is a cardinal feature of neoliberal thinking …" (7).

Neoliberalism, according to Harvey (2007), requires a state apparatus "whose fundamental mission [is] to facilitate conditions for profitable capital accumulation on the part of both domestic and foreign capital.… The freedoms it embodies reflect the interests of private property owners, businesses, multinational corporations, and financial capital" (7). To this end, neoliberal reforms in the West involved the weakening of labor power, such as unions that act as "civil society actors" and challenge the state's erosion of employment rights: "the neoliberal state is necessarily hostile to all forms of social solidarity that put restraints on capital accumulation. Independent trade unions or other social movements (such as the municipal socialism of the Greater London Council Type) … have therefore to be disciplined" (Harvey 2007, 75).

Yet, those labor unions in Eastern Europe that appeared poised to successfully challenge a government that stood in the way of multinational corporations and international trade were encouraged by neoliberal activists. Neoliberalism welcomed forms of social solidarity that would facilitate the accumulation of capital. Thatcher preached the neoliberal "liberation of entrepreneurial freedoms" when she met with members of the Solidarity movement in Gdansk, Poland, in 1988. Video footage of Thatcher's visit and later interviews with those who met with her during this visit contribute to the backdrop of the 2002 documentary *Commanding Heights: The Battle for the World Economy*, based on the book by Daniel Yergin and Joseph Stanislaw (2002). Transcripts of these scenes highlight how difficult it becomes to discern neoliberalism from civil society in the 1980s:

> NARRATOR: [Solidarity leader] Lech Walesa climbed the shipyard gate to announce a momentous victory. The workers had forced the government to recognize Solidarity, the free labor union. "I declare the creation of a free union of workers. We now have the right to strike." … When Thatcher visited Poland in 1988 she demanded that the Communist government allow her to meet Lech Walesa.
>
> LECH WALESA: You didn't say no to Mrs. Thatcher. No one refused her, so her noticing us and demanding a meeting with me and the others, that was a crucial event.
>
> CHARLES POWELL: She came into the city of Gdansk onboard a small ship, and as she went past the shipyards, all the cranes on the dockside was lined

with shipyard workers, all cheering and waving, and one began to sense here was an extraordinary experience in the making....

NARRATOR: At the house of Walesa's priest, Margaret Thatcher met with the leaders of Solidarity. A Solidarity cameraman recorded this historic meeting—and Mrs. Thatcher arguing that economic freedom and personal freedom go hand in hand.

MARGARET THATCHER: If you have a free society under a rule of law, it produces both dignity of the individual and prosperity.... How do you see the process from where you are now to where you want to be? Because whatever you want to do, it's not only what you want to do, but how the practical way you see it coming about, if you were to write down the 10 steps, from where you are now to where you want to be....

LECH WALESA: Without this meeting, there would not have been no victory, that's for sure. There would have been delay, greater difficulties, or even our destruction.

NARRATOR: Thatcher's free-market message seemed to offer an escape from a Polish economy that was debt-ridden and riddled with shortages. (Public Broadcasting Service, 2002a)

In stating that there would have been no victory without Thatcher, Walesa had credited one of the staunchest advocates of neoliberalism with the success of one of the most celebrated civil society movements.

Neoliberal reformers took a very different view of the labor unions in Britain when they opposed Thatcher's neoliberal reforms, which were based in the philosophy of economist Friedrich von Hayek. In the East, labor unions opposed an anti-neoliberal state. In the West, labor unions opposed a neoliberal state. Labor unions in Poland were celebrated by neoliberals as evidence of the realization of civil society. In contrast, labor union movements in the West were not framed as civil society movements, but as barriers to freedom and the success of neoliberal reforms. Civil society protests in Britain were quickly dismissed by Thatcher:

NARRATOR: They called it the Winter of Discontent. It seemed as if everyone was on strike.

MAN: I think it stinks, like all the other damn strikes in this country run by the filthy Socialist Communist unions....

MARGARET THATCHER (interviewed in 1993): The spirit of enterprise had been sat upon for years by socialism, by too-high taxes, by too-high regulation, by too-public expenditure. The philosophy was nationalization, centralization, control, regulation. Now this had to end.

NARRATOR: Thatcher squeezed government spending and cut subsidies to business. Thousands of bankruptcies and higher unemployment followed. Many saw her as uncaring. Britain had rarely been so divided.

CROWD OF PROTESTERS: Maggie, Maggie, Maggie. Out, out, out!

MARGARET THATCHER: Those who urge us to relax the squeeze, to spend yet more money indiscriminately in the belief that we'll help the unemployed and the small businessman, are not being kind or compassionate or caring. I have only one thing to say: U-turn if you want to. The lady's not for turning. (Public Broadcasting Service, 2002b)

Union movements that pushed alongside neoliberal politicians to open markets were characterized as civil society movements pushing for democratic reform; union movements that pushed for social rights against neoliberal reforms were characterized as barriers to democratic reform.

Although neoliberal reforms disempowered labor in the West during the 1980s and 1990s, scholars were observing the democratic potentials of civil society in the East. At the forefront were Andrew Arato and Jean Cohen (1988) who argued, based on their empirical observation of citizen resistance movements in Eastern Europe, that civil society was "more than a slogan" and ought to be "revived" by contemporary democratization projects (40). In their attempt to position civil society within a critical framework, Arato and Cohen cautioned that "anyone who wants to utilize the concept of civil society faces a double task. First, one must demonstrate the continued normative and empirical relevance of the concept to modern social conditions. Second, one must account for the negative dimensions of contemporary civil societies while showing that these are only part of the story, not the whole" (41).

In spite of Arato and Cohen's cautionary note regarding the need to account for the negative dimensions of civil society, the concept was, in most circles, uncritically received. By 1993 Craig Calhoun observed of the phrase that it was "on the lips of foundation executives, business leaders, and politicians; it seems as though every university has set up a study group on civil society…" (267). It remains true today, as Calhoun observed in 1993, that civil society is "invoked without sorting out whether it means Milton Friedman's capitalist market policies or social movements like Solidarity or the sort of 'political society' or 'public sphere' beloved of thinkers from Montesquieu to Tocqueville to Habermas …" (267). It is this conceptual black hole that allows for neoliberal reforms to piggyback on the success of the Solidarity movement, as though cherry-picked union movements and neoliberal reforms together represent the triumph of civil society over the state and not the triumph of the market over the right to well-being.

As the phrase took hold during the 1990s, academic journals began publishing debates on the topic of civil society. In 1990 *Public Culture* featured an exchange between Charles Taylor (1990) and Partha Chatterjee (1990). Like other scholars writing at this time, Taylor observed the resurgence of the ideal of civil society following the Solidarity movement in Poland and noted that the phrase was being employed in its "Hegelian" sense of a sharp distinction between the state and civil society. "Civil society in this sense exists over and against the state, in partial independence from it" (1990, 95). Taylor argued that the Eastern European movements were modeled after what their leaders assumed was an existing civil society in "the West"—"viewed from inside those Leninist societies, 'civil society' was alive and flourishing in the West ... in using the term, Eastern Europeans wanted to invoke something of the history and practice of the Western democracies as a model" (96).

Taylor's assumption that Eastern Europeans were "looking up to the West" is a gross generalization about an enormous and politically varied territory and also a dismissal of a deeply rich tradition of philosophical scholarship and discourse in the Soviet Union. However, his point that civil society in the West is not as simple as a division between the state and civil society is an important one. "Yes, there is in Western societies a web of autonomous associations, independent of the state, and these have an effect on public policy. But there has also been a tendency for these to become integrated into the state ..." (96). This is an important observation; however, Western societies are equally likely as, if not more likely than, Eastern European society to assume that civil society in the West is alive and flourishing.

The tendency for civil society to be integrated into the state to which Taylor refers in 1990 would eventually become known as "network governance." This tendency is discussed by Taylor in the context of a political philosophy known as corporatism, which was prevalent in some post–World War II welfare states in Europe and involved governing through partnership, often between trade unions, corporations, and the government (see Esping-Andersen 1990; Schmitter 1974). It is worth noting Taylor's (1990) observation of the varying relationships between the state and civil society as a potential insight into the emergence of network governance, which I explore further in Chapter Five. Taylor identifies three senses of civil society:

> 1. In a minimalist sense, civil society exists where there are free associations, not under tutelage of state power. 2. In a stronger sense, civil society exists only where society as a whole can structure itself and co-ordinate its actions through such associations which are free of state tutelage. 3. As an alternative or supplement to the second sense, we can speak of civil society wherever the ensemble of associations can significantly determine or inflect the course of state policy. No-one can deny that civil society exists [in the West] in the minimal sense ... or that it was lacking under Leninism.... (98)

In fact, many would deny claims made by Western observers of Eastern European society under Leninism; the West knew, and probably still knows, very little about everyday life in the Soviet Union. Yet, it was very quick to impose Western models of democracy through exchange programs and grants for "civil society building" efforts (Kovryga and Nickel 2004, 2006). During my participation in one such effort in 2006 I gave a lecture in Russia on the topic of NGOs in civil society. During the question period a student raised his hand and asked, "Isn't this just global hegemony?" Perhaps we should not be so quick to assume that Eastern European society looks to the West for models of civil society or that Eastern Europe does not have a strong tradition of questioning the state.

Civil society at this point becomes Westernized in the sense that the tradition of civil society in "the West" is portrayed as a "solution to" an Eastern European tradition, about which the West knows very little. Indeed, Chatterjee's (1990) response to Taylor (1990) highlights how the distinction between the state and civil society, and the failure to discuss the relation of these spheres to the market, reifies Western European notions of how human beings should be organized:

> One can see how a conception of the state-civil society relation, born within the parochial history of Western Europe but made universal by the global sway of capital, dogs the contemporary history of the world. I do not think that the invocation of the state-civil society opposition in the struggle against socialist-bureaucratic regimes in Eastern Europe ... will produce anything other than strategies seeking to replicate the history of Western Europe.... The provincialism of the European experiment will be taken as the universal history of progress; by comparison, the history of the rest of the world will appear as lack, of inadequacy—an inferior history. (131)

Chatterjee's argument brings into view how the celebration of "Poland's civil society movement" is simultaneously a celebration of the "triumph of capitalism over communism." The celebration of civil society in this context becomes conflated with the celebration of the opening of markets for foreign investment.

The debate over the importance of civil society as a lens through which to think about politics continued when in 1993 the *British Journal of Sociology* published an exchange between Krishan Kumar and G. A. Bryant. Kumar (1993) expressed caution about the usefulness of civil society—an "archaic concept" (392)—as a practical ideal in the present and argued that rather than focus on civil society, we ought to focus on the state: "If we are concerned about the abuses of state power, with recognizing and promoting pluralism and diversity, with defending rights and enabling individuals to act politically, what is wrong with the language and terms of such concepts as constitutionalism, citizenship, and democracy?" (391). In response, Bryant (1993) argues that giving priority to the state over civil society "tips the balance too far in the direction of the state" (400).

In 1995 Mark Neocleous commented on the *BJS* exchange in "From Civil Society to the Social." Neocleous disputes Kumar's interpretation of the concept of civil society in the work of Marx and Hegel, arguing that the question is not whether to emphasize the state *or* civil society; the emphasis on civil society is simultaneously an emphasis on the state. Neocleous notes that: "What also follows from the understanding of civil society in Hegel and in Marx is that one cannot conceptualize civil society without the state; to talk of civil society without the state is an absurdity" (397). Furthermore, Neocleous's discussion emphasized Hegel's concerns about relations of power in civil society:

> Civil society is actively shaped and ordered by the state. For Hegel state and civil society are structurally integrated with each other in a series of interlocking mechanisms. Thus whilst state and civil society are held apart conceptually they are simultaneously pulled together through a dual mechanism, each element of which operates in the opposite direction to the other: This interpretation of state and civil society follow from Hegel's understanding that the system of needs does not and cannot exist in a vacuum free from "interference" by public authority.... (397)

The *ordering of civil society by the state* is of critical concern; it was precisely this activity that Thatcher was engaged in when encouraging Solidarity members in Poland, as well as when condemning civil society movements in Britain.

Toward the end of the 1990s civil society was described as "paradoxical" (Foley and Edwards 1996; Alexander 1997). In their attempt to draw out this paradox, Foley and Edwards distinguished between "Civil Society I" and "Civil Society II." They use Civil Society I to refer to the concept as it is rooted in Alexis de Tocqueville's 1835 *Democracy in America,* which is still widely referenced by nonprofit scholars today. Although I simplify their nuanced discussion, Civil Society I refers to the tendency of theorists, such as Robert Putnam, who coined the regrettable phrase *social capital,* to conceptualize civil society as the horizontal development of associations outside of the state through which "civic engagement" can be practiced. Civil Society II refers to the employment of civil society "in formulating a strategy for resistance to Poland's communist regime in the 1980s ... [and] lays emphasis on civil society as a sphere of action that is independent of the state and that is capable— precisely for this reason—of energizing resistance to a tyrannical regime" (38–39). For Foley and Edwards (1996), the paradox stems from the fact that proponents of civil society want "to have it both ways" (45): Civil society should facilitate the *stability* of a democratic state through civic solidarity achieved when citizens associate through varying voluntary organizations, producing "democratic effects of association" (Warren 2000, 60–93); at the same time, it should cultivate the political impulse to *destabilize* tyrannical governments.

If the concept of civil society in the 1980s and 1990s was paradoxical, neoliberalism quickly provided a logic through which the irresolvable could appear to be resolved. The Solidarity movement in Poland might have represented a resurgence of civil society as citizen politics against the state, but it also represented a ready answer for neoliberal reformers, such as Thatcher, who benefited from the appearance of a civil society movement challenging the same government that neoliberal theorists opposed. In Chapter Seven I demonstrate how the convergence of neoliberal government reforms on behalf of open markets with the supposedly civil society-based resistance to governments that protected closed markets is paralleled in the convergence of "economic development" and "human rights."

"The Answer Is NGOs"

The scholarly debate over the concept of civil society during the 1980s and 1990s was critical in the sense that it brought into to focus the contestability of the phrase and offered conceptual tools for thinking about the relationship between civil society and the state. However, this critical inquiry is nearly absent from subsequent efforts to operationalize civil society during the 1990s, as nongovernmental organizations (NGOs) came to replace "Poland" as evidence of a robust civil society. Today, in many circles to say that the answer is civil society is also to say that the answer is NGOs. Even critical theorists such as Michael Hardt and Antonio Negri (2000), who have been credited with writing the "modern-day Communist Manifesto," seem enthralled with global civil society/NGOs: "The newest and perhaps most important forces in global civil society go under the name of non-governmental organizations (NGOs). The term NGO has not been given a very rigorous definition, but we would define it as any organization that purports to represent the People and operate in its interest, separate from (and often against) the structure of the state ..." (312–313).

Like civil society, NGO tends to be employed to describe whatever legitimating "fact" successful governing requires at a particular point in time; as Shamima Ahmed and David M. Potter (2006) point out, "scholars tend to define them in ways that suit their particular research agendas ..." (8). NGO is often used interchangeably with international nongovernmental organizations (INGOs), nonprofit organizations (NPOs), private voluntary organizations (PVOs), or civil society organizations (CSOs). NGOs are identified at least as early as 1946, when the United Nations Charter adopted the phrase to describe "any international organization which is not established by inter-governmental agreement" (in Ahmed and Potter 2006, 8; see Boli and Thomas 1999 for a detailed history). Ahmed and Potter add to the UN definition that an NGO "cannot be profit-making; it cannot advocate the use of violence; it cannot be a school, a university, or a political party; and any concern for human rights must be general rather than restricted to a particular communal group, nationality, or country" (8).

Civil society gradually became synonymous with NGOs, or the third sector. Increasing the number of NGOs came to be understood as "essential" to democratization projects: "American assistance to civil society rests on two taken-for-granted assumptions: (i) civil society is primarily embodied in NGOs, and (ii) because civil society is a prerequisite of democracy, NGOs are indispensable for democratization" (Aksartova 2006, 16). As NGOs took on an aura of legitimacy, "civil society building" was replaced by "NGO-ing" (Hilhorst 2003). This trend prompted Neera Chandhoke (2003) to declare that, "people struggling against authoritarian regimes had demanded civil society; what they got instead were NGOs!" (9).

The emphasis on NGOs as the embodiment of civil society can be partially explained by the fact that, in order to fit civil society to funding objectives, "a truly post-national global perspective and process of mapping had to be initiated" and the normative basis of civil society that informs earlier debates was explicitly rejected as being nonoperational (Taylor 2010, 3). In 1999 Lester Salamon and his research team on the Johns Hopkins Comparative Nonprofit Sector Project capitalized on this need when they produced a report titled "Global Civil Society: Dimensions of the Nonprofit Sector" (Salamon, et al. 1999), tacitly arguing that to understand the nonprofit sector is to understand global civil society. The report begins with the observation of a growing interest in a "set of institutions" known "variously as the 'nonprofit,' the 'voluntary,' the 'civil society,' the 'third,' or the 'independent' sector …" (3). Completely stripping civil society of its normative dimension, Salamon and his team of researchers define global civil society as being equivalent to the nonprofit sector, which, according to their framing, is a set of institutions (nonprofits/NGOs). Repeating Salamon and Anheier's 1996 definition of nonprofits, in the 1999 report these institutions are defined as sharing the following common features:

- *Organizations,* i.e., they have an institutional presence and structure;
- *Private,* i.e., they are institutionally separate from the state;
- *Not profit distributing,* i.e., they do not return profits to their managers or a set of 'owners';
- *Self-governing,* i.e., they are fundamentally in control of their own affairs; and
- *Voluntary,* i.e., membership in them is not legally required and they attract some level of voluntary contribution of time or money. (Salamon, et al., 3–4)

For Salamon, *civil society* is interchangeable with *nonprofit sector* and *third sector* (Salamon 2010, 169), the size of which can be determined by counting the number of NGOs in a given territory, such as a nation-state. Social economists call these measures "proxies." Researchers assume, for instance, that the number of NGOs in a country is an indicator of the health of civil society. NGOs, which often are government actors, thus become equated with civil society simply through their identification by those who study civil society. By treating NGOs as proxies for civil society, they are able to declare that "civil society is big!" and that we are "witnessing a global association revolution!" In this type of research, the number of NGOs doing government work becomes a proxy for a robust civil society: More governing outside of government becomes equated with more civil society. By 2010 it is difficult to locate a distinction between reports detailing the number of NGOs/NPOs and declarations of the robustness of civil society.

In reducing civil society to a set of counting criteria (Stone 2002), Salamon's definition of civil society has contributed significantly to the instrumentalization of the concept in the interest of governing. These counting criteria lend themselves easily to "grant outcomes and reports," which require quantifiable outputs. Although it might be difficult to "fund civil society," which, in its critical sense, rarely has a bank account, organizations with an "institutional presence and structure" can be funded and therefore held accountable for pursuing governing objectives. As Sada Aksartova (2006) details, "once the abstract concept of civil society was linked to a concrete and familiar organizational form, foreign aid donors set about disseminating professional NGOs on a large scale ... thereby further boosting the legitimization of NGOs as *the* embodiment of civil society" (18–19).

Knowledge Production and Governing: From Civic Culture to Global Civil Society

The organization of academic labor around the topic of civil society has its roots in the Cold War organization of academic labor around "political systems" and "civic culture." In the years up to the publication of Gabriel A. Almond and Sidney Verba's (1963) *The Civic Culture* (c. 1941–1946), Almond "became one of the hundreds of bees who found themselves in the dozen or so agencies that were in need of 'intelligence.' The demand for 'intelligence' as a governmental function on a large scale was something radically new" (Eulau, Pye, and Verba 2003, 467). The demand for intelligence was not radically new; Clyde Barrow (1990) identifies the marriage of the "public interest" and the university earlier, during World War I, referring to it as the establishment of "a military-academic complex." "Public service was institutionalized in research and manpower training programs that would promote capitalist economic development and in assigning intellectuals responsibility for defending the American state against internal and external threats to its legitimacy" (Barrow 1990, 124–125). In any case, knowledge production has been central to the practice of governing in the twentieth century.

Almond would continue to produce governing "intelligence" throughout his career, funded not only by the government, but also by nonprofit foundations concerned with governing:

> The major foundations Carnegie, Rockefeller, and Ford had become aware of the need for advanced and sophisticated social science research, and for the training of social scientists.... In the fall of 1953, the Council asked Almond to organize a new SSRC [Social Science Research Council] committee to work on bringing the behavioral approach [so named by the Ford Foundation] to the study of comparative politics.... Almond quickly organized the new Committee on Comparative Politics with a double mandate: first, to mobilize all the powers of the modern social sciences including in particular the insights and findings of sociology, anthropology, and social psychology for the comparative study of political systems; and second, to expand the range of comparative analysis to include the non-Western world, and in particular, the new states just emerging from colonial rule. (Eulau, Pye, and Verba 2003, 468)

Almond had established, at the urging of these foundations, a "micro-apparatus of truth generation" (Luke 1989b, 137).

Building on Foucault's understanding of the way in which knowledge functions as power, Luke (1989b) sought to understand how the academic production of the concept of civic culture functioned as discipline, which is to say that it governed in the interest of stability. In his genealogy of the political culture concept as it was advanced by Almond and Verba, Luke (1989b) explored how social science was engaged in culture/political socialization through the production of power/knowledge (135). "Learned treatises on 'the arts of government,' like Almond and Verba's *The Civic Culture* and *The Civic Culture Revisited* are not simply academic exercise existing *in vacuo*. Both works are grounded in the post-1945 East–West struggle over creating stability and instability ... both works assess the unity of employing *survey techniques* to study citizen attitudes and values within a set of quite varied nations to deal with the macropolitical problem of *democratic stability*" (Luke 1989b, 137). Governing knowledge stabilizes by "taking account of" and thus takes account of that which needs to be stabilized.

The pursuit of knowledge in this way is as political as that which it observes, continually adapting its ways of knowing to the requirements of governing. In his 1991 APSA Presidential Address Theodore J. Lowi (1992) argued that political scientists "become what they study."

Thus, as the state underwent technocratization and sought to "predict in order to control" (3), social scientists in turn developed methods, or ways of knowing, that were "consonant with bureaucratic thinking" (3). This is demonstrated in Timothy Mitchell's (1991) discussion of the abandonment of the state as a conceptual variable in the 1950s in favor of the "political system." Political scientists, including Almond, argued that the state was too vague and not broad enough to include other societal actors—actors that must be known in predictable ways in order to be controlled. The boundary between the state and society was rejected as a useless distinction in favor of the political systems approach (Mitchell 1991, 78–79). Almond (1988) argued that the concept of the state should be replaced by "political system," which "included the phenomena of the state—legally empowered and legitimately coercive institutions—but also included these new extralegal and paralegal institutions of political parties, interest groups, media of communication, as well as social institutions such as family, school, church, and the like, insofar as they affected the political process" (855). The political system provided a basis for expanding knowledge about the population and thus contributed to the expansion of governing. Governing, for Almond, required more knowledge about what we today call civil society; we might think of the "political system" as "governance" and of "parastatal" or "extrastatal" institutions as "civil society actors."

Mitchell (1991) points out that the rejection of the state concept was part of a broader societal shift in which U.S. political science research became organized around the needs of U.S. political power: "Postwar comparative politics, according to Loewenstein, would have to relinquish its narrow concern with the study of the state in order to become 'a conscious instrument of social engineering'. . . . This instrument would be used for 'imparting our experience to other nations and . . . integrating scientifically their institutions into a universal pattern of government' . . ." (79). In order to achieve this goal, "Almond sought additional foundation funds for a competitive program of grants to individuals for field work" (Eulau, Pye, and Verba 2003, 468). Social scientists involved in this production of knowledge about subjects (people who are governed) and subjectivities (the "proper" disposition of people who are governed) belong to a regime of power/knowledge (Foucault 1980). For Foucault, the better that subjects are "known" and "knowing," the more efficiently they are governed, or disciplined. Thus, to "know" civil society as a territory with a set of accepted "good practices" or a level of "performance" is also to make available categories that help to produce "the emergence of population as datum, as a field of intervention and as an objective of governmental techniques" (Foucault 1991, 102) and to know civil society according the same epistemology as the state and the market is to bring it into the realm of knowing/governing.

The practices involved in "knowing the political system" or "knowing civil society" belong to what Foucault (1980) called the ensemble of knowledge practices that support governing and which are *themselves governed*. The interaction of scientific "truth statements" and power explains why at some points in time academic labor seeks to know the truth about communism and why it sometime seeks to know the truth about civil society in former communist countries. Power extracts legitimacy from knowledge, and thus power *needs* scientific truth statements. These scientific truth statements are pursued not only by the state, but also through "grants"; this is to say, power often pays for the pursuit of knowledge that facilitates its initiatives. For the Ford Foundation (2010), a "grant is a commitment by the foundation to make payments to an organization or an individual over a set period of time to further the work of one of our initiatives." The Ford Foundation (2010) initiative to build "democratic and accountable government" indicates that they need to know and do more about "increasing civic and political participation, strengthening civil society, promoting electoral reform and democratic participation, promoting transparent, effective and accountable government, and reforming global financial governance." Participation (an indication that we accept that we are legitimately governed), civil society, and finance contribute to a single initiative: stability (see Roelofs 2009).

Universities encourage the academic labor they employ to supplement the university's budget and research profile through the pursuit of these types of "funded research," which are usually tied to governmental objectives. Luke (2005) explains, "bodies of knowledge with perceived fundable potential, interdisciplinary fundability or existing rankable luster typically are valued over those without high fundability, interdisciplinary openness, or potential for greater luster in national rankings" (19). In some disciplines a grant from the Ford Foundation is valued more highly than a publication: Instrumental knowledge that contributes to stabilization is valued over critique that would contribute to transformation. Funded research does not always, but certainly has the potential to, produce its own impact on the "rules of knowledge formation." Almond waited sixty years to publish his dissertation research because "Professor Merriam, concerned about offending some of the major New York donors to the University of Chicago, refused to recommend its publication" (Eulau, Pye, and Verba 2003, 467).

The pursuit of "sponsored" or "funded" research involves matching one's research objectives to the objectives of the government or foundation to which one is applying. Frequently, these grant objectives become institutionalized within the university as "centers" and "institutes," which often employ grant writers, such as those produced by the emergent public sociology programs discussed in Chapter Two. These grant writers are responsible for pursuing further funding and sponsored research. Sponsored research involves securing contracts to produce what Burawoy (2005a) calls "policy sociology." Grants for international development work, such as "building civil society in developing countries," often require a plan for institutionalization of the funder's objectives, such as the establishment of centers in the country in which one is imparting the funded knowledge. Grant proposals thus typically include strategies for "sustainability": One must demonstrate that the center has a plan in place to continue to operate once the funding ends. In other words, the recipient must demonstrate how they will continue to pursue the initiatives of the grant maker in the absence of funding.

Governments and foundations who give "grants" to academics are making knowledge purchase requests of academic labor. Their demands for knowledge are also demands for intellectual authority, for a standard of normality, for confirmation that a crisis requires attention: in short, for evidence of a basis for a governing intervention. Academic labor thus becomes organized around the objectives of governing, as in the establishment of the Committee on Comparative Politics during the Cold War and the study of "civic culture." Following the end of the Cold War the objectives of governing shifted. The breakup of the Soviet Union had to be explained as a triumph of democracy, but also as a fragile triumph in need of stabilization, which could be achieved through research into "civil society." Civil society offered an additional conduit for governing through the establishment of NGOs, which could receive funding and engage in practice outside of formal state boundaries.

The Cold War emphasis on civic culture has been replaced with the contemporary emphasis on global civil society as "answer" to the problems of democratic stability—as in Kaldor's (2003) *Global Civil Society: An Answer to War.* Social science is engaged now, like Almond and Verba were then, in "creating a micro-apparatus of truth" that, to the extent that it is successfully transmitted as "freedom and individual liberty," functions to discipline potential ruptures in stability. Government agencies in the United States, such as the United States Agency for International Development (USAID), and foundations, such as the Ford Foundation, began to offer grants to university researchers who wrote proposals that successfully demonstrated how they would use grant monies to "build" global civil society.

Global civil society is explained by Manuel Castells (2008) as resulting from a shift in debate about public affairs from the national to the global level. Castells begins his case for global civil society with the following distinctions:

> The public sphere is an essential component of sociopolitical organization because it is the space where people come together as citizens and articulate their autonomous views to influence the political institutions of society. Civil Society is the organized expression of these views; and the relationship between the state and civil society is the cornerstone of democracy.... It is through the public sphere that diverse forms of civil society enact this public debate, ultimately influencing the decisions of the state.... (78–79)

The underlying concern here is with the stability of public affairs and thus with how civil society can stabilize and legitimate the actions of the state. Castells argues that the new global sociopolitical order requires a global civil society in order for "global actors and institutions to interact in a nondisruptive manner, the same kind of common ideational ground that developed in the national public sphere should emerge" (80). Like Hardt and Negri (2000), Castells is taken with the NGO aura, noting that they "have considerable popularity and legitimacy" (84–85). Whereas Hardt and

Negri provide no support for their assertion of NGOs as the most potent force in global civil society, Castells's support for this observation is based on the following:

> *The Global Civil Society Yearbook* series, an annual report produced by the London School of Economics Centre for Global Governance and under the direction of Mary Kaldor, provides ample evidence of the quantitative importance and qualitative relevance of these global civil society actors and illustrates how they have already altered the social and political management of global and local issues around the world (e.g., Anheier, Glasius, and Kaldor 2004; Anheier, Glasius, and Kaldor 2005; Anheier, Glasius, and Kaldor 2006). (84)

The Global Civil Society Yearbook series to which Castells refers is produced by the London School of Economics Centre for the Study of Global Governance, one of a global ensemble of university-based centers that produce knowledge about global civil society (see Taylor 2010). I will further examine the type of knowledge produced by these centers in Chapters Six and Seven; for now, however, I want to focus on the evidence that serves as the basis for Castells's observation of the legitimacy and popularity of NGOs and their production of global civil society: *The Global Civil Society Yearbook*.

The Global Civil Society Yearbook 2004/2005 presents much like the annual report of a private corporation. It is heavy, the pages are colored and glossy, and the text is accompanied by photographs of crowds of people holding placards around the globe, participating in what we are to assume is civil society. Of the 375 pages, pages 225–335 are tables of data measuring the following:

- the global economy
- global trade
- transnationality of top 100 transnational corporations
- trafficking in persons
- air travel and international tourism
- media and communication
- governance and accountability
- ratification of treaties
- social justice, defined as "the realisation of economic rights" (270)
- corruption
- refugee populations and flows
- peacekeeping
- environment
- number of NGOs in countries and cities
- country participation in INGOs
- links between international organizations

- meetings of international organizations
- NGOs by purpose
- employment, volunteering and revenue of NGOs
- political rights and civil liberties
- tolerance
- attitudes toward globalization
- attitudes favoring Americanization (225–335)

As Mitchell (1991) observes of Almond and Verba's *Civic Culture, The Global Civil Society Yearbook* seeks "to 'codify' not just the formal institutional rules of the state but the 'subtler components' that formed its 'social psychological preconditions'—that combination of democratic spirit and proper deference toward authority…" (80).

These tables impose upon global civil society what Foucault (1995) discussed as discipline:

> it fixes; it arrests or regulates movements; it clears up confusion; it dissipates compact groupings of individuals wandering around the country in unpredictable ways; it establishes calculated distributions … to form a body of knowledge about these individuals, rather than to deploy the ostentatious signs of sovereignty. In a word, the disciplines are the ensemble of minute technical inventions that made it possible to increase the useful size of multiplicities by decreasing the inconveniences of power which, in order to make them useful, must control them. (219–220)

The Global Civil Society Yearbook 2004/2005 tracks the movement of bodies as refugee population flows, and air travel tracks the possible organization of resistance counterpower in NGOs, and measures resistance to globalization and Americanization.

This methodology is continuous with the "formal techniques of survey research [as the] new technologies of discipline and surveillance that bring political life into the realm of explicit calculation and create knowledge-power to transform society" (Luke 1989b, 132) that prevailed during the Cold War. *The Global Civil Society Yearbook* documents attitudes toward Americanization and globalization as a measurement of "democratic global civil society." This is precisely the same type of scholarly research sought after by government agencies in the Cold War era, which Luke (1989b) details as the creation of an apparatus of truth:

> in the July 1984 *American Political Science Association Personnel Service Newsletter,* a notice from the United States Information Agency (USIA) advertised employment in an "applied setting" for a "Social Science Analyst-Latin American Branch", who "will design and analyze sample surveys of Latin American elite and general public opinion on ideas relevant to U.S. foreign policy…". (133)

In explaining why such truth generation emerged as a social science discourse, Luke (1989b) argues that the "system of democracy, development, capitalism and freedom produced by power in the West seeks normalizing control and disciplinary tools to maintain itself, contain the Soviet bloc, and expand abroad …" (134).

The evidence for global civil society, if we begin with Castells's (2008) argument and examine the evidence to which he refers, is composed of primarily data about globalization and surveys about attitudes. This biopower, as Luke (1989b) argued of the civic culture surveys, "brings to life both of these new entities, making the psychic state of the citizen (as revealed in attitudes and values), and the political culture (as typified by model distributions of attitudes and values), objects of explicit calculation … 'working democracies' constitute a normal population which is a controlled distribution of qualities and traits, restructuring the image of 'how much of what' must be present to make an individual or a nation fit into the empirical grid of normalized expectations" (138–139).

Knowledge about civic cultures and civil societies takes account of that which must be governed—deviance from the "correct" attitudes toward globalization and American foreign policy. Yet, it is not only the collection of "knowledge about" that governs. Surveys have spillover effects. Gouldner (1970) explained that surveys are themselves embedded in a logic control: "Stated otherwise, information-gathering systems or research methods always premise the existence and use of some system of social control. It is not only that the information they yield may be used *by* systems of social control, but that they themselves *are* systems of control. Every research method makes some assumptions about how information may be secured from people and what may be done with people, or to them, in order to secure it …" (50). For Gouldner (1970), "the conventional methodologies of social research often premise and foster a deep-going authoritarianism, a readiness to lie to and manipulate people: they betray a bureaucratic numbness" (50).

With nearly twenty-five pages of similar data tables further dispersed throughout the *Yearbook*, approximately 40 percent of the book is made up of numbers. This charting of the social space available for politics into positivist knowledge makes *an ontological claim* (Agger 1989b). The *Yearbook* charts a social ontology based on the epistemology of instrumental rationality, implicitly arguing that we can observe civil society by counting states, markets, and surveyed social patterning. These figures "frame the problem [in order to] present a lawful account of the social world" (Agger 1989b, 14). Through the use of charts, the *Yearbook* transforms what Agger calls *science aura* into a civil society aura: "the embellishment of the text with design, figure, and number, which in effect become texts themselves. When the prose lacks a certain authority … figure steps in to win the day" (1989c, 70). *The Global Civil Society Yearbook* leaves little text to be contested, counting on the reader not contesting the authority of the figure. This is problematic because, as Agger points out, science aura results in a public less likely to identify and confront the politics of figural representation.

The Institutionalization of Civil Society as Third Sector Research

As civil society replaced civic culture as the basis of political stability, knowledge production once performed by public administration scholars involved in the Comparative Administration Group (see Garcia-Zamor and Khator 1994; Loveman 1976) and political scientists involved in Almond's Comparative Politics Committee (see Mitchell 1991, 79; Eulau, Pye, and Verba 2003) became involved in "third sector research." Much like social science researchers "took account" of civic culture, third sector research "takes account" of civil society. Rupert Taylor (2010) explains that "to date, the central task for scholars working in the field has been to delineate the composition, scope, and structure of the third sector and to map the field, first nationally and then—with the impetus of *Voluntas* [*International Journal of Nonprofit and Voluntary Organizations*], The Johns Hopkins Comparative Nonprofit Sector Project, and the International Society for Third Sector Research (ISTR)—cross-nationally and globally" (1).

While both "comparative politics" and "third sector research" produced governing knowledge, third sector research not only took account of "political systems," it also fit neatly with neoliberalism. Third sector research originated at the same time that Hayek's neoliberal philosophy was beginning to take hold in the United States and Britain. Olaf Corry (2010) traces the phrase "third sector" to Amitai Etzioni's 1973 article in *Public Administration Review*, titled "The Third Sector and Domestic Missions" (13). Etzioni's argument for the third sector is a thinly veiled argument for privatization of state enterprises:

> It seems that enough is known for us to be able to state now that greater reliance on the third sector, both as a way of reducing government on all levels and as a way of involving the private sector in the service of domestic missions, would be significantly more effective than either expanding the federal or other levels of government or dropping them on the private sector. (322)

In 1973, the third sector, as it was defined by Etzioni, referred to enterprises like the Federal National Mortgage Association (the now infamous Fannie Mae) and the Communications Satellite Corporation (321–322). This privatization strategy evolved into the "hollow state" (Milward and Provan 2000) and eventually "network governance." As civil society became conflated with the number of NGOs, and the number of NGOs increased to meet the needs of neoliberal strategies of privatization, which devolved government services to NGOs in the form of grants, it became possible to declare that there was a surge in civil society during an era of neoliberal governance and that, as Salamon (1994) argued in his observation of "a global 'associational revolution'," this was a reflection of the "long-simmering crisis of confidence in the capability of the state" (109).

As civil society began to appear in the funding schemes of foundations, national governments, and international governing organizations, Salamon, who is director of the Johns Hopkins Center for Civil Society Studies, began to operationalize and institutionalize the concept. Like Verba, Salamon directs a university-based center dedicated to comparative research on a global scale. (See Taylor 2010 for further examples of institutionalization.) The Center for Civil Society Studies is situated within the Johns Hopkins Institute for Policy Studies, further collapsing any former conceptual distinction between the state and "civil society" and positioning their practices within the broader framework of the transformation of the state thesis, as well as what Burawoy calls "policy sociology."

The Center for Civil Society Studies has harnessed participants in more than forty countries, often including national governments, to apply government resources to their projects. Like Burawoy, Salamon often invites "local" academics to participate in his projects, which in turn provides them with publication opportunities, which in turn serves to further embed the appearance of the project's validity. At the conclusion of these projects, Salamon often attends an invitation-only "launch" of the report, attended by government officials, NGO leaders, local academics who participated in the project, and the media. This was the case in New Zealand in 2008, when the Office of the Community and Voluntary Sector (OCVS), then positioned within the New Zealand Ministry of Social Development, partnered with the Center for Civil Society Studies to produce *The New Zealand Non-profit Sector in Comparative Perspective* (Sanders, et al. 2008) and *Counting Non-profits in New Zealand*. The research team found that there were 97 thousand nonprofit institutions operating in New Zealand in 2005. According to Salamon's research assumptions, this number indicates a healthy democracy with a large civil society. Of these 97 thousand nonprofit institutions, 45 percent were culture, sports, and recreational nonprofit institutions (Statistics New Zealand 2005). Although this might be an indication of a high level of social capital (Putnam 2000), it hardly brings to mind the images of the Polish Solidarity movement.

Just as Burawoy's portrayals became quickly institutionalized within the ASA and university programs, Salamon's portrayals have been quickly institutionalized in New Zealand. With some qualifications, Salamon's definition is the official definition of the nonprofit sector in New Zealand: OCVS "adopted the description used by the Johns Hopkins Centre for Civil Society Studies, however New Zealand also has unique features such as the place of Mâori organisations within the sector" (OCVS 2010). The OCVS also promotes his work on their Web page: "While in New Zealand, Lester Salamon gave a number of presentations about the work of the Center for Civil Society Studies of the Johns Hopkins Institute for Policy Studies. You can download his presentations here." According to Burawoy's definition, Lester Salamon might be a very successful global policy sociologist.

Public Sociology and Civil Society? Public Sociology and NGOs?

Recall that in his argument for public sociology, Burawoy declared that the standpoint of political science is the state, the standpoint of economics is the economy, and the standpoint of sociology is civil society. It seems reasonable to inquire, therefore, whether to argue today that the standpoint of sociology is civil society is also to argue that the standpoint of sociology is governance through NGOs. Yet, this is a somewhat redundant question, given that the institutionalization of public sociology has involved a "skill set" dedicated to the performance of the "nonprofit sector." As I detailed in Chapter Two, the curricula of emerging public sociology programs include governance, evaluation, organization and management of groups, and performance. Institutionalized in this way, public sociology joins the third sector research regime, which has been framed in significant ways by Salamon and Anheier and the Johns Hopkins Comparative Nonprofit Sector Project (Taylor 2010, 2). Rupert Taylor's observation that third sector research has been dominated by value-neutral approaches is certainly correct (Taylor provides an excellent history of the field). However, it is also true that as funding for "civil society NGOs" emerged, a parallel scholarship began to do legitimation work involving the portrayal of NGOs as accountable governing actors. These analytical inquiries into accountability question whether or not NGOs are legitimate democratic actors (Ebrahim 2003, 2009; Ebrahim and Weisband 2007; Edwards and Hulme 1996; Jordan and Van Tuijl 2006; Najam 1996).

Although much of the legitimation work done on behalf of non-state actors takes place within the governance literature, which I address in Chapter Five, because the third sector relies heavily on contracts and grants, accountability has emerged as a significant theme. As a broad concept, Michael Edwards and David Hulme (1996) define accountability as "the means by which individuals and organizations report to a recognized authority (or authorities) and are held responsible for their actions" (967). These authorities, according to Adil Najam (1996), can include: NGO accountability to patrons; NGO accountability to clients, and NGO accountability to themselves (341). In practice, Alnoor Ebrahim (2003) identifies five mechanisms of NGO accountability, many of which appear nearly verbatim in the public sociology curricula: disclosure statements and reports; performance assessment and evaluation; participation; self-regulation; and social auditing. In a later piece, Ebrahim (2009) identifies the three normative logics of NGO accountability as governance, performance, and mission (887).

However, to promote accountability is not necessarily to promote civil society. Neera Chandhoke (2003) observes that the exogenous funding regimes to which NGOs often belong

> breeds its own troublesome trajectories. First, NGOs spend so much time on accounting for money, or reporting how it was used to the donors, that they are left with little time for the people for whom the money was meant in the first place. Secondly, the way in which most NGOs solicit and receive funds from external sources leaves them vulnerable to external controls. It also leaves them with little leverage to contribute to the development of civil society by empowering people to voice their own demands and make claims on the government. (72)

Counting, categorizing, and legitimating NGOs is good academic business these days, but it is hardly "a critical standpoint."

NGOs should not be assumed to be democratic actors simply by virtue of being counted as a proxy for civil society (Chandhoke 2003; Harvey 2007; Hayden 2002; Hilhorst 2003; Kamat 2003; Rodriguez 2007; Smith 2007), nor should they be assumed to be democratic by virtue of being accountable. NGOs have been accountable to what many would consider to be undemocratic neoliberal governments. As Andrea Smith (2007) points out, NGOs have been used by capitalist interest and the state

> to monitor and control social justice movements; divert public monies into private hands through foundations; manage and control dissent in order to make the world safe for capitalism; redirect activist energies into career-based modes of organizing instead of mass-based organizing capable of actually transforming society; allow corporations to mask their exploitive and colonial practices through "philanthropic" work; encourage social movements to model themselves after capitalist structures rather than to challenge them. (3)

This is a deeply problematic observation when considered in the context of public sociology programs dedicated to training students to evaluate performance, which is another way of saying "monitor and control" NGOs. Whether or not 1989 was a transformative moment in the history of civil society, we must now read appeals to civil society for what they disguise. Although their circulation through various knowledge networks creates a sense of actuality, the phrases *public sociology, civil society,* and *nongovernmental organization* falsely imply clear institutional boundaries as well as boundaries of practice. To understand public sociology and civil society in relationship to governing thus requires that we understand the relationship between civil society and that state, which I turn to in Chapter Five.

Chapter 5

The Transformation of the State Thesis

The academic distinction between the state and civil society has eroded significantly over the past two decades as many who previously explained the state and civil society as distinct spaces have come to advocate a form of governing known within varying academic disciplines as governance, which involves the state partnering with so-called civil society organizations. The expansion of governing into "civil society" has ushered in widespread celebrations of transformation: globalization, global civil society, cosmopolitanism, and increased "development." Within this cacophony of celebration an allied transformation of the state thesis has proposed that we have entered an era in which power is competitively distributed through post-liberal democratic governance networks. In this chapter, I outline the transformation of the state thesis, focusing specifically on "radically democratic network governance" (Sørensen and Torfing 2005a). I locate this thesis within the post-Marxist knowledge regime and demonstrate how its institutionalization has contributed to the expansion of instrumental practices of governing in a neoliberal era rather than to "the radical democratic governance" that it claims to observe.

A Note on Liberalism-Post-Liberalism

In order to understand the radical post-liberal break claimed by network governance theorists,[1] it helps to understand the logic of legitimacy that preceded their declaration. Liberalism, a theory of the state, is known in the field of public administration as "constitutionalism." Constitutionalism is generally associated with John Rohr's (1986) *To Run a Constitution: The Legitimacy of the Administrative State.* (Also see Wamsley and Wolf 1990.) In spite of recent declarations of "post-liberalism," which is the theory of the state that underpins the transformation of the state thesis, Rohr's theory of liberal constitutionalism remains a stabilizing concept in the field of public administration. As recently as 2010 Stephanie Newbold made a renewed argument for the constitutional perspective, "constitutional tradition and rule of law should serve as the foundations of public administration scholarship in the United States.... Without the acceptance of this norm, American public administration will find itself unable to embrace the intellectual underpinnings that legitimate the field in its entirety" (538).

Constitutionalism, for public administration, provides an answer to what this field discusses as "the legitimacy question," which prompts scholars of public administration to explain the practices of the state as democratic, while preempting attempts to address the potential *illegitimacy* of the state. The logic of constitutionalism goes like this: Legitimate state action is based on the Constitution; those who wrote the Constitution, although they did not specifically mention public administration, implied it in several places, and it also came up in their debates about what how the state ought to be organized; therefore, public administration is a legitimate actor in our democratic state. Rohr's definition of the administrative state is:

> the political order that came into its own during the New Deal and still dominates our politics.... Its hallmark is the expert agency tasked with important governing functions through loosely drawn statutes that empower unelected officials to undertake such important matters as preventing "unfair competition," granting licenses as "the public interest, convenience or necessity" will indicate, maintaining a "fair and orderly market," and so forth.... Despite its warts and wrinkles, it has provided the underpinnings of a free, decent, and prosperous society most Americans have enjoyed for the past half-century. I want to legitimate the American administrative state because I believe it provides the stability to accommodate orderly change in a liberal democratic regime that is fundamentally just. (xi)

Rohr's assumption that the U.S. administrative state is fundamentally just, or that most Americans have enjoyed prosperity for the past half century, is, like Burawoy's (2005a) organic division of labor for sociology, an ontological fiction.

In spite of the continued stabilization of the liberal state's knowledge practices, Eva Sørensen (2002) identified four challenges to constitutional liberalism represented by a shift to network governance: "'the people' as a pre-given entity; representation as the link between 'the people' and decision makers; the administration as a non-actor in democracy; and the institutional separation of the political system and society" (694). It is important to note that the transformations referred to by Sørensen (2002) are not necessarily transformations of the powerful epistemological practices of the state, but rather are transformations of the constitutive logic of the state; Sørensen's call to constitute network governance as legitimate governance according to the logic of post-liberalism, like Rohr's and Newbold's calls for constitutionalism, is what Philip Abrams (1988) calls "legitimation work":

> what is being legitimated is, we may assume, something which if seen directly and as itself would be illegitimate, an unacceptable domination. Why else all the legitimation work? The state, in sum, is a bid to elicit support for or tolerance of the insupportable and intolerable by presenting them as something other than themselves, namely, legitimate, disinterested domination. (76)

Network governance scholars claim to observe a post-liberal era of governance, but remain engaged in constructing an answer to public administration's legitimacy question. Sørensen and Torfing (2005a) make an extensive effort to demonstrate that network governance is *generally accepted by the state*, in particular because it *reduces resistance* to policy (205). This echoes Rohr's legitimizing statement twenty years earlier. In their acts of legitimation, Rohr, Newbold, Sørensen, and Torfing are involved in the same activity. Although their conceptions of "the best way to govern" might differ, it remains true that, as Ralph Miliband (1969) argued, "the politics of advanced capitalism have been about different conceptions of how to run the *same* economic and social system" (72).

In the same way that public administration scholars achieved legitimacy for the welfare state through the declaration of the presence of "democratic scientific management" in the industrial era, network governance scholars achieve legitimacy for the neoliberal state in their declaration of the presence of "radically democratic user forums" in a post-Fordist era (Gantman 2005), while still employing the rationality of "efficiency" as a core element of democracy (Sørensen and Torfing 2005b, 214). Writing as though either industrialization or post-Fordism were organic political developments rather than logics of legitimacy, network governance theorists are able to frame the formation of "politics" in relationship with the capitalist state and its associated knowledge practices as the necessary outcome of an "inevitable" economic transformation.

The Transformation of the State Thesis

With the possible exception of the recent attempt to establish a new "Constitutional School for American Public Administration" (Newbold 2010), it is now a widely taken-for-granted and rarely contested "fact" that the global organizational landscape is shifting from government (bureaucracy) to governance (the involvement of supposedly nongovernmental organizations and citizen/users in the practice of government). Bureaucracy is now assumed to be a dying breed of organization, and networks of interdependent nongovernmental organizations are assumed to be its radical replacement. At the same time, the practices of the state that were once legitimized by the label *liberalism* are now legitimized by the label *post-liberalism* (Sørensen and Torfing 2005a), which coexists with the practices of the neoliberal state. According to these varying declarations, domestic politics are now "global domestic politics," citizen power is now "consumer power" (Beck 2005a), and government is now governance (Blomgren Bingham, Nabatchi, and O'Leary 2005; Hill and Lynn 2005; Kettl 2002; Milward and Provan 2000; Pierre 2000; Provan and Kennis 2008; Sørensen 2000, 2002, 2005, 2006a, 2006b, 2007a, 2007b; Sørensen and Torfing 2003, 2005a, 2005b, 2007a, 2007b, 2007c, 2007d, 2007e, 2008, 2009).

These concurrent pronouncements represent the transformation of the state thesis, a phrase I use broadly to describe recent declarations that the state and its associated practices have shifted from national hierarchical government to cosmopolitan and/or post-liberal governance. The transformation of the state thesis refers to the claim that there has been a shift in the boundary between the state and "non-state" spaces, with power being devolved to "non-state" actors. As a "discursive regime" (Foucault 1972) the transformation of the state thesis involves not only several narratives about a shift to governance, but also claims concerning cosmopolitanism (Beck 2005a, b; Delanty 2006) and collaborative governance (Ansell and Gash 2008; Donahue 2004; Newman, et al. 2004; Sirianni 2009; Zadek 2008). Although these narratives reinforce each other, in this chapter I am specifically concerned with the thesis that we have entered an era of network governance and with the idea that this represents a "radical transformation" (Sørensen and Torfing 2005a). This thesis is most fervently advanced by Eva Sørensen and Jacob Torfing (2005a, b), who fashion "radically democratic network governance" in the form of: "a relatively stable horizontal articulation of interdependent, but operationally autonomous actors; who interact through negotiations; which take place within a regulative, normative, cognitive and imaginary framework; that to a certain extent is self-regulating; and which contributes to the production of public purpose within or across particular policy areas" (2005a, 203; 2005b, 197). In spite of their (2005b) declaration that democratic standards must remain "ungraspable" and "contingent" (211), Sørensen and Torfing (2005a) claim that these "governance networks are here to stay. They have become a necessary ingredient in the production of efficient public governance in our complex, fragmented and multi-layered societies" (197).

The transformation of the state thesis begs an ontological question that must be addressed before proceeding. Within what space is the state's epistemology practiced, and within what realm is it experienced? For that matter, what *is* the state? Liberalism in political science belongs to "the statist" approach, from which the political systems advocates (Almond and Verba 1963), discussed in Chapter Four, claimed to depart. This approach to studying the state, as Mitchell (1991) points out, relies on a definite boundary between state and society (86). For Mitchell, neither approach recognizes that the "boundary of the state (or political system) *never marks a real exterior.* The line between state and society is not the perimeter of an intrinsic entity, which can be thought of as a free-standing object or actor" (90). We can position Mitchell's argument that the "statist approach always begins from the assumption that the state is a distinct entity, opposed to and set apart from a larger entity called society ... in fact the line between the two is often uncertain" (89) against the distinction between the state and civil society upon which public sociology and, in its reference to the state in relationship to "non-state" spaces, network governance rely.

The transformation of the state thesis, although it claims to observe "a shift," still depends on this line between state and society having existed in the first place in order to observe its transformation. Its reference point is the state, and its observation is of a transformation in the boundary of the state. In this way, it already is a statist approach; it originates within a conception of the boundary between state and society; it is a thesis about the movement of the boundary of the state, and if we accept that this boundary has been *radically transformed* in the interest of "more democracy," then we must first accept that it existed as a "less democratic" boundary in the first place. We cannot simultaneously propose that the state has "radically" transformed "beyond" liberalism and also neglect *how* it was that liberalism existed to be radicalized.

In attempting to understand the *transformation* of the state, we are confronted with the same problem that Abrams (1988) confronted when describing the study of the liberal state, which is that it defies scrutiny by avoiding the particulars of practice (60). Abrams observed that:

> The state emerges from these studies as *an ideological* thing. It can be understood as the device in terms of which subjection is legitimated ... it presents politically institutionalized power to us in a form that is at once integrated and isolated and in satisfying both these conditions it creates for our sort of society an acceptable basis for acquiescence.... We are in the world of myth.... Myth is of course a rendering of unobserved realities, but it is not necessarily a correct rendering. (68–69)

Abrams proposes to abandon the study of the state as a material object, but to continue to study "the state idea" (75). The state is more than an idea; it is also the rendering of an idea into practice, which is organized through institutions. However, Abrams's state idea (the legitimacy question) highlights how legitimation often shrouds practice. The transformation of the state thesis renders unobserved realities into a basis for legitimation. To say that the state is an ideological thing is to say that it is an ontological portrayal of the legitimate organization of power. Thus, when Sørensen and Torfing (2005a) advance "the legitimacy question of post-liberalism" they are engaged in giving us "an account of political institutions in terms of cohesion, purpose, independence, common interest and morality without necessarily telling us anything about the actual nature, meaning or functions of political institutions" (Abrams 1998, 68).

The thesis of a transformed state repackages for a better fit with neoliberalism and global capitalism a set of assumptions that, from the perspective of critical theories of the state, have long been questionable. Critical theorists of the state never assumed the "non-state" spaces—variously called "civil society," the "third sector," or the "voluntary sector"—to be a space free from the exercise of state power. (See Aronowitz and Bratsis 2002; Barrow 1993; Foucault 1991, 1995; Mandel 1972; Mitchell 1991.) Thus, the starting point for the transformation of the state, like Burawoy's (2005a) starting point for public sociology, begins from an ontological fiction. If we assume that a boundary between the state and society exists, then we are able to declare its transformation, which in turn orders our reality. On the other hand, if we assume that there never was a firm boundary between state and society (Mitchell 1991), what we witness is not a transformation of the state, but a transformation of the ordering logic of state theorists. Although theorists of the transformation of the state make sweeping claims about the radicalization of power, they rarely consider their own political act of claim-making as part of this enterprise.

A related problem is that discussions of network governance as a transformation of relations of power neglect that the history of mainstream modern organizational practice is *not* primarily a history of shifting contracts between supposed sectors, it is *not* primarily a history of phases of nonparticipation and participation, and it is *not* primarily a history of shifting shapes in chains of command. The primary history of mainstream modern organizations is instead a history of instrumental rationality, or control and economy achieved through productive knowledge (Clegg 2009; Denhardt 1981; Foucault 1980; Gantman 2005; Horkheimer and Adorno 1989; Lyotard 1984; Smith 1990; Weber 2007). Clegg's examination of the foundations of organizational power suggests that "even when it appears to be most absent, power is always most present; we see this especially in the slippage of everyday organizational life" (56). My inquiry into the transformation of the state thesis questions the legitimizing assumption that relations of power in the organization of the state have been radically transformed in a shift from government to governance.

That the transformation of the state thesis belongs to the practice of legitimation work is also demonstrated by observing its parallel with the rise of neoliberalism as a set of assumptions about the purpose of knowledge in relationship to governing. As Harvey (2007) succinctly, though not apologetically, explains, according to neoliberal theory, "the neoliberal state should persistently seek out internal reorganizations and new institutional arrangements that improve its competitive position as an entity vis-à-vis other states in the global market" (65). A neoliberal state and a transformation of governance exist in tandem because governance depends on the state devolving responsibility. Jon Pierre (2000) describes neoliberalism as an impetus for governance:

> For Reagan, Mrs. Thatcher, Mulroney, and their ideological followers … the recipe to alleviate these problems was a firm monetaristic economic policy coupled with deregulation, privatization, drastic reductions in the civil service, the introduction of "managerialism" in the public sector, and a profound institutional restructuring of the state creating semi-autonomous agencies to replace governmental centers of command and control functions. (1–2)

Without explicit consideration of *this* concurrent transformation, the celebratory declaration of a newly transformed and democratic state emerges as a legitimating logic for what is still the neoliberal state. As Harvey (2007) notes, "behind these major shifts in social policy lie important structural changes in the nature of governance. Given the neoliberal suspicion of democracy, a way has to be found to integrate state decision-making into the dynamics of capital accumulation and the networks of class power that are in the process of restoration …" (76).

The *legitimacy of* and the *epistemological necessity for* the neoliberal transformation of the state are blurred and asserted through the declaration that the world is too complicated for us to govern in any other way. Goldsmith and Eggers (2004) explain the transition to governance as resulting not from political agency but from "increasingly complex societies [that] force public officials to develop new models of governance … twenty-first century challenges and the means of addressing them are more numerous and complex than ever before" (7). Read critically, this statement of the necessity for the neoliberal transformation of the state from government to governance also argues that the practice of governing is the practice of knowing, and that the aims of governing-by-knowing are efficiency and the stabilization of security. These claims are highly contestable (Foucault 1995; Marcuse 1966). Complexity, efficiency, and security through alternative state structures does not represent an epistemological break from previous forms of governing, because epistemology is still aimed at the management of complexity, the achievement of efficiency, and the profitability of nature, which the Frankfurt

School recognized as the essence of instrumental rationality and domination and Foucault (1991, 1995) recognized as characteristic of liberal forms of governing.

The underlying rationale of the necessity for the expansion of governing practices is that the world has become too complex, and thus governing must change in the interest of efficiency and stabilization. Complexity and the associated practices of governing are not irrefutable facts. Modern-day complexity resulted from a series of epistemological *choices* involving "the dissolution of myths and substitution of knowledge for fancy" (Horkheimer and Adorno 1989, 3). Complexity was born of the choices made by human beings to employ knowledge as a form of power, to govern the world completely (Horkheimer and Adorno 1989, 3–4). Complexity and the authority of the practices that it brings forth govern as "complementary 'discursive formations' [that] always already presume 'consursive formations' in their production, consumption, reproduction, circulation, and accumulation of meaning, value, or work" (Luke 2003, 102). Complexity as the legitimating condition for the emergence of network governance, which is just "more governing in more places," involves the denial that we can transform the circumstances that govern our lives because these circumstances are too complex to be within our control. As the Frankfurt Institute for Social Research (1972, 148) argued,

> modern society is blamed with being too "complicated".... It is questionable whether any such complexity in an actual sense is really present ... there is grounds for the suspicion, that the case is not so much that the matter itself is complicated, but that the separation of functions in a society based on the division of labor has also taken hold of the knowing subjects, and has confined these to such an extent to specific, mainly technical, practical tasks, than an insight into the whole is hardly available to them any longer....

Complexity as a necessity for limiting the "realm of the possible" is not radical or democratic (Frankfurt Institute for Social Research 1972, 149). Complex, fragmented, and multilayered are not formations that exist in an atmosphere beyond everyday practice: We can reach them, impact them, and change them. They are alterable institutionalizations, but to the extent that they are portrayed as something outside of our reach, they function on behalf of the present by slicing up the political world into a portrayal of accessible and inaccessible pieces and substituting a new and "inaccessible" explanation of legitimacy for the decreasingly previous explanation of legitimacy. Circumstances that seem inaccessible are in fact encoded with knowledge, value, and *choices,* and thus they are open to revision according to *alternative* understandings of knowledge and value.

Network governance might in fact exist in practice as an increase in partnerships between organizations and people who previously did not directly interact or partner to deliver services. However, as I demonstrate in Chapter Six, network governance has not stopped organizations from budgeting, counting, measuring, producing, and aiming to do these things in the most "rational, efficient, and productive" ways possible. Indeed, for many, rationality and efficiency are *better* achieved through governance than through government (Goldsmith and Eggers 2004; Kettl 2002; Sørensen and Torfing 2005a, b), and socially concerned organizations are increasingly encouraged to focus on counting and economy (Mook, Quarter, and Richmond 2006; Mook 2010).

A Note on Post-Marxism

Like public sociology and civil society, the ideal of radical democratic network governance has been institutionalized within a particular knowledge regime. Sørensen and Torfing's thesis on post-liberal radically democratic network governance belongs to a theory of politics known as post-Marxism, which is most often associated with Ernesto Laclau and Chantal Mouffe. Laclau and Mouffe's *Hegemony and Socialist Strategy: Toward a Radical Democratic Politics* and Mouffe's *The Return of the Political* seem to occupy an uncontested position as the "radical theory books" in the governance, administration, management, and policy literatures.[2] The excitement surrounding Laclau and Mouffe's work as a basis for the "radical democratic nature" of contemporary governing, which I argue is not the least bit radical, is hard to ignore. It is therefore difficult to fully engage with contemporary statements on governing if one does not first address post-Marxism. (For lucid explorations of post-Marxism, see el-Ojeili 2001; Tormey 2001; Townshend 2004.) This fact alone is telling of the legitimating relationship, intentional or not, that post-Marxism has in relationship to governing. Curiously, to borrow a phrase used by Fredric Jameson (1984) to describe postmodernism, in its institutionalization post-Marxism acts as "the political logic of late capitalism."

I want to note at the outset that, although it is not possible to fully consider "radically democratic network governance" without also considering its main referent—post-Marxism as it is expressed by Laclau and Mouffe—I strongly suspect that the work of Laclau and Mouffe enjoys what Gouldner (1970) called the halo effect, or deviance credits granted to an author due to their prestigious title or university affiliation:

> When a scholar is confronted with a very prestigious colleague's work, which he finds difficult to understand or to see the importance in, he is more likely to blame *himself* than when confronted with similarly obscure work by a less prestigious colleague…. Faced with the obscure work of prestigious colleagues, scholars are also likely to favor it with the assumption that its manifest muddiness is indicative of a hidden depth…. Because of its difficulty the work must

> be given an "interpretation." … The result, then, is that the new doctrine is protected by becoming deeply internalized in each adherent and by developing the social solidarity of the first-generation "seed-group." (201–202)

These seed groups, having made a significant investment in an idea, have a vested interest in its institutionalization. It is, at the least, true that post-Marxism has been widely institutionalized within the contemporary governance literature.

I also want to note that, although they claim to have made a radical break, many of Laclau and Mouffe's observations were made years earlier by Western Marxists, phenomenological Marxists, and feminists who were influenced by what are called postmodern and post-structural ideas (see Agger 1991b), while still maintaining the critical perspective that there is nothing radically democratic about the present. As Steven Best and Douglas Kellner (1991) note, "Laclau and Mouffe fail to observe that critiques of reductionism, essentialism, and teleological visions of history and the proletariat have already been made within the Marxist tradition" (201). These critiques are not as difficult to understand as many post-Marxists would have us believe them to be. In short, it is now widely recognized that class/labor cannot explain all power relations; liberalism is no longer the dominant idea in the legitimation of the state; our identity, what theorists call subjectivity, is fluid and is a site of politics and power; language is political; and ontology is an important category of critique. In short, the economy cannot explain everything, and thus we ought to focus critique on other political spaces, such as identity, language, and ontology. Most critical theorists today would agree with Laclau and Mouffe that the economy does not explain *everything*, but would argue that this does not mean that it should be excluded from critique; it still explains some things.

In the case of the transformation of the state thesis, post-Marxist thought joins the ensemble of governing knowledge by providing legitimation of the idea that current formations of governing are radically democratic. The "post-Marxist" observation that has been most successfully institutionalized as a governing idea is "post-liberalism," which originates as a critique of liberalism. This critique, which, for many, is influenced by the work of philosopher Jacques Derrida, is based in the recognition that ontology is political and proposes that, as an ontological claim, liberalism functions politically as it constitutes social relations. This insight is not exclusive to post-Marxism as Laclau and Mouffe expressed it in 1985. In 1982 Michael Ryan published a book titled *Marxism and Deconstruction: A Critical Articulation,* in which he argued that:

> Liberalism's transcendence of difference remains theoretical; it cannot allow any political position to be realized that is not itself liberal, in other words, that

> does not rest upon the celebration of the plurality of positions. It is here that
> the coercive core of liberal generosity makes itself felt. Liberalism seems to
> mandate nothing, but in fact it does nothing but mandate itself: one *must* be
> universally inclusive and accord privilege to all political positions. This seem-
> ingly general inclusion is at the same time a universal exclusion, excluding any
> specific position ... because such a position cannot attain the transcendental
> generality and disinterested inclusivity of liberalism.... Liberalism has no
> outside, because it is itself outside play.... (122)

In other words, liberalism portrays the political world as a space in which
everyone has an equal opportunity to advance their positions, but liberalism
has already structured the rules of the game in such a way that one cannot
oppose liberalism itself. This is important because the liberal ontology makes
claims to democracy that preserve what are often deeply undemocratic practices. The crux of the argument is that, in its portrayal of politics, liberalism
excludes all other political positions while claiming to be democratically
inclusive.

I do not dispute that the ontology of liberalism is political. However,
beyond this recognition, I depart from Laclau and Mouffe's politics. They
have displaced the liberal *ontology* only to turn around and stabilize the
epistemological practices of the state. In her critique of deliberative democracy,
which she incorrectly conflates with liberalism,[3] Mouffe (1999) argues that
"far from being merely empirical, or epistemological, the obstacles to the
realization of the ideal speech situation are ontological" (751). What she
fails to recognize is that ontology *is empirical* to the extent that ontology
is a governing idea. Further, ontology is *stabilized by epistemological claims to
governing*, such as complexity. We cannot displace governing ontologies without also displacing epistemological practice. This was recognized by Ryan
(1982) when he argued that "breaking the logic of power in theory (which
is also in the practice of reading, interpreting, and knowing) is where the
immediate effectivity of deconstruction resides. Deconstruction makes one
aware of how theory is determined in practice, as well as how practice can
be produced by theory" (173).

Throughout the 1990s Mouffe attempts to *fit* the democratic ontological
revolution claimed in *Hegemony and Socialist Strategy* to the undemocratic
epistemological practice of politics. Following the publication of Laclau and
Mouffe's *Hegemony and Socialist Strategy*, Mouffe translates post-Marxism's
position on post-liberalism into a legitimation of contemporary practices
of governing, which serves the same function as public administration's
"legitimacy question"—on what basis is the state a legitimate democratic actor? As in Rohr's (1986) argument for the legitimacy of the liberal state and
Thatcher's argument for civil society (Public Broadcasting Service 2002a),
this is accomplished through an observation of the present practice of governing being founded in a "democratic regime that is fundamentally just."

Mouffe's (2005) explanation of the present as "radically democratic" provides a legitimating narrative for "radical democratic network governance." In other words, if the present is radically democratic, then so, too, are present formations of governance.

This portrayal is constructed by Mouffe (2005) in the first two pages of *The Return of the Political,* where she echoes the tone of Thatcher's speech to leaders of the Solidarity movement in Poland (Public Broadcasting Service 2002a). She begins by declaring that: "it is indeed the political which is at stake here, and the possibility of its elimination" (1). The "impotence" of most political theory, she argues, could "jeopardize the hard-won conquests of the democratic revolution" (2). Although it is unclear through what action this conquest was achieved and therefore what present the declaration of its arrival stabilizes, what was conquered, or how it could have emerged from an absence of politics that requires her to return us to the political, we are presented with the contemporary political moment as characterized by a democratic revolution.

The practice of Mouffe's call for post-liberal pluralism fits neatly with neoliberalism's dismantling of the welfare state by delegating what were once the "liberal state's" responsibilities to "extra-state" institutions, such as private companies that contract with government, nongovernmental organizations that contract with government, and private philanthropists who do state work (Nickel and Eikenberry 2010). Neoliberalism, after all, is not at all dependent on liberal political philosophy; it fits equally well, if not better, with post-liberal political philosophy, which poses *no* challenge to neoliberal governance, which sustains the *epistemological power* of the state in late capitalism even as it redistributes the practice of power.

Mouffe (1999) rejects "deliberative democracy" as being based in a liberal ontology and antagonistic pluralism. Her alternative, agonistic pluralism, is based on a distinction between "the political" and "politics"—"By 'the political,' I refer to the dimension of antagonism that is inherent in all human society, antagonism that can take many different forms and can emerge in diverse social relations. 'Politics,' on the other hand, refers to the ensemble of practices, discourses and institutions that seek to establish a certain order and to organize human coexistence in conditions ..." (754). Politics, she argues, tries to create unity out of conflict—to discipline it (754). This creates a problem, Mouffe argues, as Ryan (1982) did, because this unity can never be achieved. Therefore, "what is at stake is how to establish the us/them discrimination in a way that is compatible with pluralist democracy" (755). In other words, what is at stake is the preservation of pluralist democracy—its legitimation.

The problem, she argues, as Foucault did, is that power is not an external relation. This is to say, we internalize the objectives of power and govern ourselves in the absence of its physical presence. Most critical theorists will grant that power is not an external relation, but to neglect its empirical practice, as Mouffe (1999) does when she narrowly frames it as an ontological problem stemming from liberal politics, is to put the question of power outside the realm of politics. As Foucault (1980) notes, "the way power was exercised—concretely and in detail—with its specificity, its techniques and tactics, was something that no one attempted to ascertain; they contented themselves with denouncing it in a polemical and global fashion as it existed among the 'others', in the adversary camp" (115–116). Mouffe is not critical of the *exercise* of power through practice; her aim is to stabilize power relations by rewriting the ontological logic of governing, which, in turn, provides a legitimating logic for the contemporary distribution of power. Her solution to Foucault's recognition of the non-externality of power is to find a way to *legitimate* it by *fitting* it into the political system that stems from very political ontology that she claims is false. Agonistic pluralism requires us to "acknowledge the existence of relations of power and the need to transform them, while renouncing the illusion that we could free ourselves completely from power, this is what is specific to the project of 'radical and plural democracy' that we are advocating" (Mouffe 1999, 753).

Although she does not explicitly state that she is employing Foucault's analysis of power, Mouffe's analysis needs to be distinguished from Foucault's project in order to retain his insight into power as a non-external relation as a potential *critique* of post-Marxism and its "proximity" to the practices of governing. In arguing that power was not external, Foucault (1995) was not arguing, as Mouffe (1999, 752) does, that power was ineradicable. Although it is possible that he believed this to be true, his project was not to demonstrate the ineradicability of power and thus provide a stabilizing logic for present formations of governing. Foucault (1995) historically located the emergence of disciplinary power in a period of governing during which, in order to make the population *useful,* power had to be made more efficient. In other words, Foucault's historical analysis of disciplinary power in no way supports the idea that freeing ourselves of power is an illusion; it demonstrates the historical, and thus alterable, formations through which disciplinary power emerged and how it was practiced. Foucault's analysis of power certainly was not, like Mouffe's, a call to "make power relations compatible with pluralist democracy." On the contrary, I would argue that Foucault's project would be to locate Mouffe's "agonistic pluralism" in relation to contemporary demands of governing. Foucault's point was that we should reveal the relationship between knowledge and oppressive power relations, not that we should find a better way to institutionalize them.

Theories of politics, such as post-Marxism, are explanations of how power is distributed among governments, citizens, nonprofit organizations, and profit-seeking institutions. However, these theories of politics are still only stories about necessity and possibility that are transmitted into authoritative knowledge. As Gouldner (1970) and Foucault (1980) note, their success can be considered in light of their positioning within ensembles of power and the value that they achieve by virtue of knowing/rendering the present as permanent or knowing/rendering it to be alterable. It is thus important to keep in mind that *explanations* of governing are also *instruments* of governing. Governing involves the rendering of knowledge and its epistemological *practice* as authoritative, the portrayal of the ontological versions of the world that such practices stabilize as fixed, and the portrayal of this intersection as legitimate, legitimately democratic, and legitimately permanent by virtue of being *known as such.*

The Institutionalization of Post-Marxism as Radical Democratic Governance

Post-Marxism as a portrayal of "the political" is institutionalized as a legitimate governing practice by "radical democratic governance scholars." Most notably, Torfing, of the post-Marxist "Essex School"[4] and director of the Centre for Democratic Network Governance (CDNG) in the Department of Society and Globalisation at Roskilde University, with Sørensen has worked extensively to translate post-Marxism into practice via the governance literature that emerged in tandem with neoliberalism. Between 2000 and 2009 Sørensen and Torfing published no fewer than sixteen articles, chapters, and books articulating post-Marxism and Mouffe's so-called post-liberal version of the political under the label "radically democratic network governance" (Sørensen 2000, 2002, 2005, 2006a, 2006b, 2007a, 2007b; Sørensen and Torfing 2003, 2005a, 2005b, 2007a, 2007b, 2007c, 2007d, 2007e, 2008, 2009).

The idea of a radically democratic transformation of the state is repeatedly expressed by Sørensen and Torfing, who have declared that the world has entered an era of "radical democratic network governance." This language echoes Laclau and Mouffe's (2001) so-called post-Marxist move "towards a radical democratic politics." Although the idea began to circulate as early as 2000, in 2005 Sørensen and Torfing published "The Democratic Anchorage of Governance Networks" and "Network Governance and Post-liberal Democracy." Both articles begin by declaring that politics has changed and the state has transformed and both articles advance Sørensen and Torfing's (2005a, b) definition of "radically democratic network governance," referenced previously.

To begin, Sørensen and Torfing (2005b) provide a definition of governance networks as a horizontal articulation of self-regulating actors who negotiate within a common framework of understanding to produce public purpose (197) and a declaration that these networks are permanent and necessary in order to achieve efficiency in societies that are complex and fragmented. With this "fact" established, both articles are then dedicated to fitting this power formation to a logic of democratic legitimacy. In "Network Governance and Post-liberal Democracy" Sørensen and Torfing (2005a) credit post-Marxist post-liberalism with being able to resolve the question of democratic legitimacy posed by network governance: "it should now be clear, the choice between liberal and post-liberal theories of democracy determines the response to the question of the democratic problems and potentials inherent in governance networks" (227). Elected politicians and post-liberals, they explain, do not view network governance as a challenge to democracy, but rather "render it possible to see how governance networks might contribute in new and important ways to organizing and regulating processes of democracy in our complex, differentiated and multi-layered societies" (227–228). In the same way that it is difficult to challenge the logic of liberalism, it is difficult to challenge their logic of post-liberalism because, like liberalism, it places any potential oppositions outside the realm of critique: If liberalism cannot explain network governance as democratic, then post-liberalism can. The critical question, however, is whether or not providing an alternative explanation of something renders it democratic in practice. As I explain in Chapter Six, there is a difference between rendering it possible to explain something as democratic and rendering it possible in practice.

At this point, we have a definition of governance networks and a declaration that they are permanent and necessary in order to produce efficiency in societies that are complex and fragmented and also a theory that explains it as democratic. Next, Sørensen and Torfing (2005b) develop a model for the "democratic anchorage of governance networks." The governance network is said to be democratically anchored when it:

- is controlled by democratically elected politicians;
- represents the membership basis of the participating groups and organizations;
- is accountable to the territorially defined citizenry; and
- follows the democratic rules specified by a particular grammar of conduct. (201)

Although the democratic grammar of conduct is a post-Marxist theme (Mouffe 2005), in a dizzying twist for the logic of post-liberal democracy, Sørensen and Torfing (2005b) have proposed to anchor the democratic legitimacy of the governance network in the state, which Mouffe (1999) rejects as liberalism (754). In addition to reasserting the liberal themes of representation and a territorially defined citizenry, Sørensen and Torfing (2005b) propose that "politicians should play a key role in the efforts to improve the democratic anchorage of governance networks … it is the only group that we can hold directly responsible for the eventual lack of democratic anchorage" (215).

Of course, we hold politicians directly responsible through the instruments of liberalism: constitutions, courts, and elections. According to this logic, post-liberal network governance is going to hold liberalism accountable for the failures of post-liberal network governance.

Although they claim to depart from traditional liberal politics, Sørensen and Torfing (2005b) assign traditionally liberal politicians to the role of "meta-governor."

> The minimum requirement is that politicians take on the task of controlling what goes on in the self-regulating governance networks by exercising meta-governance. Politicians must actively engage in the initial design of networks, in the internal decision-making processes, and in the overall framing of the policy that is produced in and by governance networks. (215)

In other words, politicians, who derive their democratic legitimacy from liberal theories of democracy, must now extend this legitimacy to the post-liberal governance networks that cannot be explained as democratic by liberal theories of democracy in order to legitimate that which is not explained by liberalism to be democratic and thus must be explained by post-liberalism. When this argument appears again in "Network Governance and Post-liberal Democracy," Sørensen and Torfing (2005a) further explain that politicians "can decide on all issues that they regard as of general relevance and importance, and leave the more specific and detailed decision making to the [self-governing] governance networks" (230).

To recap, we have a definition of governance networks and a declaration that they are permanent and necessary in order to produce efficiency in societies that are complex and fragmented, a reference to post-liberal theory as an explanation of this formation as democratic, and now these post-liberal networks are anchored in liberalism. It seems reasonable to ask, what do governance networks do? In "Democratic Anchorage of Governance Networks: The Case of the Femern Belt Forum," Torfing, Sørensen, and Trine Fotel (2009) describe a network developed around the construction of a bridge between Germany and Denmark. Interestingly, this case study is framed as an empirical test of the model that Sørensen and Torfing (2005b) built in "The Democratic Anchorage of Governance Networks." The four criteria for democratic governance networks (controlled by democratically elected politicians, representative of the membership of participating groups, accountable to territorially defined citizenry, and conforming to democratic rules) are framed as four propositions, or hypotheses, each beginning with "democratic anchorage in elected politicians can be measured by paying attention to the following norms..." (Torfing, Sørensen, and Fotel 2009, 287). In other words, the research inquiry is not concerned with what governance networks do so much as it is concerned with whether or not their model, which is based in liberalism, is valid as a means to measure democratic anchorage of post-liberal networks. Styled after positivist research articles (see Agger 1989c), roughly thirteen pages are dedicated to the authority of "methodology" and nine pages are dedicated to what took place in the Femern Belt Forum. After testing each of their hypotheses, the "*overall verdict* is that the democratic anchorage of the Femern Belt Forum is: MODERATE" (304). RADICAL was not included in the scale.

According to this analysis, the case for "radical democratic network governance" is as follows. First, governing no longer fits with the liberal ontology, and therefore it must be based instead in the post-Marxist vision of post-liberalism. We can "test the explanatory validity" of the post-liberal framework in order to judge the degree to which governance networks in practice conform to their post-liberal principles of democracy, which are rooted in liberal institutions. To sum up, we have a definition of governance networks and a declaration that they are permanent and necessary in order to produce efficiency in societies that are complex and fragmented, an analytical model that explains this formation as democratic, and "proof" that the explanation/model can be tested and operationalized, and therefore their democratic anchorage of post-liberalism can be said to be "weak, moderate, or strong." In other words, the epistemological practices of governing can be placed inside or outside the logic of post-liberalism.

The Centre for Democratic Network Governance research includes the Collaborative Innovation in the Public Sector (CLIPS), which

> refers to the creation and implementation of new knowledge and creative ideas generated through mutual learning derived from interaction between users, professionals, public administrators, politicians, consultants, interest groups and private companies. CLIPS will during the following four years identify both driving forces and barriers to collaborative innovation and develop methods for organising and managing collaborative innovation. The overall goal is to promote and advance innovation in the public sector and foster new public policies as well as to shed light on the significance of institutional design and management of innovative processes.... (Centre for Democratic Network Governance 2010)

Far from being "radically democratic," innovation is a neoliberal theme belonging to what is known as "new public management," or "running government like a business." New public management involves the commodification of citizenship, and citizenship interaction with the state is reduced to an economic exchange between customer and entrepreneur. As Janet V. and Robert B. Denhardt (2003) argue: "The common theme in the myriad applications of these ideas has been the use of market mechanisms and terminology, in which the relationship between public agencies and their customers is understood as based on self interest, involving transactions similar to those occurring in the market place. Public managers are urged to 'steer not row' their organizations, and they are challenged to find new and innovative ways to achieve results or to privatize functions previously provided by government" (549). This is what network governance institutionalized in the Centre for Democratic Network Governance "does." It is not radically democratic; it is radically neoliberal.

There is a lack of practical conflict between the neoliberal state and network governance. Harvey's (2007) description of the neoliberal state concurs perfectly with Sørensen and Torfing's (2005a, b) definition of "radically democratic network governance" as a shifting partnership and negotiation among new autonomous actors: "Neoliberalization has entailed, for example, increasing reliance on public-private partnerships.... Business corporations not only collaborate intimately with state actors but even acquire a strong role in writing legislation, determining public policies, and setting regulatory frameworks (which are mainly advantageous to themselves). Patterns of negotiation arise that incorporate business and sometimes professional interests into governance through close and sometimes secretive consultation" (76–77). Read through Harvey's lens, rather than being a radical counterforce to neoliberalism, network governance is fueled and funded by the neoliberal state. The legitimacy of neoliberalism depends on the governance network, because it is dependent on the state seeming to do less in order to portray "civil society" and the market as a space within which individuals achieve liberty and freedom.

Producing case studies of network governance and other institutionalizations of post-Marxism is good academic business these days. In her recent investigation into shifting structures of governance, Sarah Carr (2007) asserts that antagonism and passion, as they are theorized by Mouffe, are the basis for an "almost unprecedented shift in power from manager and worker to client and a major culture change in the social care system" (267). Carr instigates an important discussion about political agency when she writes that "exclusionary structures, institutional practices and professional attitudes can affect the extent to which service users can influence change" (267). However, exclusions and practices are not only structural and participatory, but also epistemological. Carr is correct that political contestation is an important consideration for governance scholars, but it also matters *what* it is that we are contesting. Carr's evidence of contestation involves policies that center "on choice and independence, and intend to give users a hitherto unparalleled degree of control.... The reforms should eventually mean that adult service users have the option to choose and purchase their own care and support" (267).

Unclear how this degree of control was practiced passionately and agonistically, I examined a copy of the report that Carr refers to as the source of an unprecedented shift in power. The report, *Independence, Well-Being and Choice*

(Department of Health 2005), emphasizes "the importance of regulation and performance management as levers for challenge and change and propose that both should be modernised to reflect more accurately the outcomes we have defined" (13). The "unprecedented shift in power" that Carr has described, detailed in Box 5-1, is no more than "user" participation in the neoliberal privatization and management of the health care system.

Whether or not there is a deliberative forum of citizens or users present in the already-determined governing process is not an appropriate point at which to theorize political agency; even if it were, the empirical practice of these "radical" shifts, as Box 5-1 demonstrates, is hardly a radical shift in power. The point at which we are able to theorize political agency is instead the portrayals that govern imagination prior to and within such a forum. If contestable portrayals fail to be deliberated because they are not recognized as such, deliberation fails to be political and instead functions to legitimate a state that is not at all transformed in practice. This is a critical point in relationship to Carr's Mouffian interpretation of agonistic transformative power relations in governance because the recognition of the *contestability* of governance must precede *conflict* over governance. Mouffe (2005) and Carr (2007, 272) want to *discipline* conflict and passion within already existing power relations. I want to *transform* already existing power relations that discipline utopian imagination.

The transformative potential of these declarations of radical network governance must be judged at the level of practice. Typically, the network is approached as a shifting structure of *hierarchy* (Goldsmith and Eggers 2004) rather than as a *relationship* of practices that can be transformed. The assumption that shifts in the shape of relations rather than the practice of

---

Box 5-1 Evidence of the Transformation of the State Thesis as an "Unprecedented Radical Transformation of Power"

The key proposals to deliver this vision include ... wider use of direct payments and the piloting of individual budgets to stimulate the development of modern services delivered in the way people want; greater focus on preventative services to allow for early, targeted interventions, and the use of the local authority well-being agenda to ensure greater social inclusion and improved quality of life; a strong strategic and leadership role for local government, working in partnership with other agencies, particularly the NHS, to ensure a wide range of effective and well-targeted provision, which meets the needs of our diverse communities; and encouraging the development of new and exciting models of service delivery and harnessing technology to deliver the right outcomes for adult social care. We would now like to hear your views on our proposals so that together we can move forward by implementing a shared vision and creating a social care environment which is right for the 21st century. (Department of Health 2005, 14)

relations is the means by which governing takes place significantly influences how we approach collective action and the potential for transformation. As Dorothy Smith (1990) notes: "Objectifying reasoning, knowledge, memory, decision-making, judgment, evaluation, etc. . . . are, of course, accomplished only by individuals in everyday local settings, who enter into and participate in objectified forms of constituting organizational and discursive relations beyond themselves" (211). This is precisely the case in exhibit one in the role of "direct payments" and "targeted interventions" as examples of our "proof" questioning the "radical" transformation of the state.

Governance scholars producing knowledge within this regime of understanding institutionalize the idea that *power has been radicalized.* Yet, Sørensen and Torfing (2005b) make explicit that disempowerment is a feature of radically democratic governance networks: "We will have to content ourselves with the critical and public engagement of mass media, scientific and professional experts, interest organizations, social movements, and other governance networks and different kinds of empowered individuals. Public audit and critical scrutiny require a certain amount of resources, capacities and political interest that we cannot commonly expect to find in unorganized groups of citizens with low education and income" (210). The requirements for the further democratic anchorage of this situation, in which we have to content ourselves with the exclusion of the disempowered, further include: "transparency, access to public dialogue with the governance network, and responsiveness on the part of the governance network" (Sørensen and Torfing 2005b, 210). Participation in this ensemble is governed by rules of conduct in which the rulers respond in "an appropriate way without scorn, ridicule or any other dismissive attitudes" and the citizens are "prepared to learn that their criticisms are ill-founded or misguided" (Sørensen and Torfing 2005b, 210). Sørensen and Torfing (2005b) are very clear that the success of this radical democratic formation of governing depends on "the crafting of social and political technologies enabling the network actors to govern themselves and others in a manner ensuring that each and everybody are governed without the excessive use of force and resources" (210). This is the efficiency of disciplinary power. Democratic legitimacy is "obtained if governance networks and the actors within them follow rules and norms inherent to a democratic grammar of conduct" (2005b, 211).

Certainly network governance is involved in the practice of governing, but the governing networks that most of us encounter in our everyday lives are of the disciplinary sort, involving social engineering commercials that tell us to manage our bodies so that we are less expensive in relationship to the state, labels referring to us as "users," admonishments to sustain consumption scientifically so that we can continue consuming, to increase our value to the economy through skill upgrading, and to be philanthropic in order to reduce the burden on the state for human well-being and make the present seem benevolent. Our participation in "radically democratic" network governance, as Sørensen and Torfing make abundantly clear, is contingent upon the internalization of the messages of disciplinary governance networks or else contentment with our lack of resources, capacities, and political interest; it is these messages, not the ontology of liberalism, that are the basis for our exclusion.

My argument thus far has been that, in their portrayals of the world and of the people who inhabit the world, intellectuals intimate the possibility of transforming the circumstances that govern our lives. Knowledge therefore always is a political statement that governs possibility in relationship to a public with whom intellectuals communicate both directly, through public speech, and indirectly, through the production of "social facts" that become the basis for governing decisions. Governing thus involves the management of these ontological and epistemological assumptions. This management is powerful to the extent that it prevents our recognition of the possibility that alternatives exist. Governing is, as Abrams (1988) observed of the state, "a triumph of concealment" (77), involving a complex of knowledge and knowledge producers (Luke 2005). If the study of the state was the production of "an acceptable basis for acquiescence" (Abrams 1988, 68), then so, too, in the contemporary moment are public sociology, civil society, and governance, all of which concern themselves with the legitimacy of the political practice of knowledge as though it were an apolitical fact.

Notes

1. *Governance* is a broader term than *network governance,* which implies governance through partnership (see Pierre 2000). I use *network governance* to refer to Sørensen and Torfing's (2005a, b) conceptualization of governance.

2. For example, in the work of: Sarah Carr, "Participation, Power, Conflict, and Change: Theorizing Dynamics of Service User Participation in the Social Care System of England and Wales," *Critical Social Policy* 2 (2007): 266–276; Thomas J. Catlaw, "Constitution as Executive Order: The Administrative State and the Political Ontology of 'We the People'," *Administration and Society* 37 (2005): 445–482; Mel Gray and Stephen A. Webb, "The Return of the Political in Social Work," *International Journal of Social Welfare* 18 (2009): 111–115; Paul Hoggett, "Conflict, Ambivalence, and the contested Purpose of Public Organizations," *Human Relations* 56 (2006): 175–194; Robert L. Ivie, "Rhetorical Deliberation and Democratic Politics in the Here and Now," *Rhetoric and Public Affairs* 5(2) (2002): 277–285; Jon Nixon, Melanie Walker, and Stephen Baron, "From Washington Heights to the Raploch: Evidence, Mediation, and the Genealogy of Policy," *Social Policy and Society* 1(3) (2002): 237–246; Lynn A. Staeheli, "Citizenship and the Problem of Community," *Political Geography* 27 (2008): 5–21; Steve Vertovec, "Minority Associations, Networks, and Public Policies: Re-assessing Relationships," *Journal for Migration and Ethnic Studies* 25(1) (1999):

21–42; and Joris Van Wezemael, "The Contribution of Assemblage Theory and Minor Politics for Democratic Network Governance," *Planning Theory* 7 (2008): 165–185.

3. I disagree with Habermas on many points, but I find Mouffe's characterization of his work as that of "a liberal deliberative democrat" to be an extraordinarily narrow reading of his work. Habermas's distinction between system and lifeworld can be read as a political critique of the ontology of the liberal capitalist state, and his early work on legitimation and rationality is especially instructive when considering post-Marxism. Furthermore, the "deliberative democrats" to whom Mouffe (1996, 1999) refers have never accepted wholesale without criticism Habermas's theory of the public sphere.

4. See Townshend 2004, 284.

Part III

Power and Practice

Only in rites
can we renounce our oddities
and be truly entired.
Not that all rites should be equally fonded:
some are abominable.

—*W. H. Auden*, Archaeology, *1973*

Chapter 6

Governing Texts

Considered together, public sociology, civil society, and governance reveal a problematic union between knowledge production and the practices of governing. If public sociology and governance involve reference to, and the institutionalization of, civil society; if civil society is produced by intellectuals as NGO management and research; and if the practices of NGOs often are indistinguishable from the practices of the state, how can we distinguish between the practices of public sociology, civil society, and governance, and how can these practices be distinguished from governing? Further, if the institutionalization of public sociology, civil society, and governance involves the practice of governing in "non-state" spaces, is this practice any different from the practices of the state prior to the transformation of the state thesis?

In this chapter I establish a textual framework for understanding how these institutionalized explanations and their associated practices can be analyzed for their common "textual form of participation in social relations" (Smith 1990, 4). I demonstrate through an analysis of the portrayal by the Johns Hopkins Center for Civil Society Studies of collective human action as a discrete economic input, how texts function powerfully as taken-for-granted encodings of value. I argue that the radicalization of power must take place not according to declarations of transformation, but through attention to the intersection of knowledge and its associated practice of value, which, following Ben Agger, Timothy W. Luke, and Dorothy E. Smith, I identify as being embedded in *texts*.

Text, Portrayal, and Power

The idea of texts as a mode of power relations draws the insights of North American critical theory, together with postmodern and post-structural theories of the text (see Agger 1991b) in order to extend criticism of what the Frankfurt School called domination. In North America, Agger, Luke, and Smith argue from varying perspectives that governing involves a powerful formation of textual relations of value. Circa 1989 Agger, influenced by the Frankfurt School and Jacques Derrida, published *Reading Science: A Literary, Political, and Sociological Analysis; Fast Capitalism: A Critical Theory of Significance;* and *Socio(onto)logy: A Disciplinary Reading.* Luke, influenced by Jean Baudrillard and Umberto Eco, published *Screens of Power: Ideology, Domination, and Resistance in Informational Society,* and Smith, influenced by Harold Garfield and Michel Foucault, published *Texts, Facts, and Femininity: Exploring the Relations of Ruling.* All three authors demonstrate how *texts are powerful portrayals of possibility;* when we fail to recognize textual portrayals of reality as being contestable authorings constructed by individuals, texts become governors of transformative imagination.

For Agger "text is that which compels or liberates behavior" (1989a, 58) and the "modal power relationship is between readers and writers" (47). In Agger's (1989a, b, c) conception the text encompasses not only words on pages, but all formations that are infused with authorial choices. The text is therefore that which encodes meaning, including the chosen formations of numbers, figures, money, and edifice. Texts that conceal the circumstances of their authorship compel behavior by governing in a "rush from page to act without detouring through mind" (Agger 1989a, 59), thus bypassing the political moment at which we might challenge the meaning that such texts assign to our lives. For Agger (1989a), those texts that reveal the circumstances of their authorship, and that they are therefore alterable, potentially liberate behavior as we mediate their meaning and challenge their inevitability. The opportunity to challenge portrayals of possibility is *the very essence of transformative politics.*

Throughout Agger's oeuvre, utopian imagination and public dialogue frame the possibility for transformative action. The decline in utopian imagination, he suggests, is due to the tendency for texts to become reified, or "thing-like"; we fail to identify that they are authored, and thus we fail to contest their portrayals of possibility and impossibility. *Recognition of textuality is essential to transformative politics,* because texts, as the articulation of a particular imagination, can be transformed. In theorizing textuality and authorship, Agger (1989a) was concerned with the decline of our awareness of textuality, the way in which texts "dominate imagination by pretending not to be written" (86). Textuality entails contestability. A decline in textuality is a decline in politics, or a decline in the ways in which people find contestable meaning and dispute their own marginalization. A decline in textuality is also an increase in domination, which takes place as a result of our failure to recognize the opportunity critically to mediate the texts that govern our lives: "texts [no longer] stand apart; they are written to be lived immediately" (Agger 1989a, 23).

For Agger, texts, especially positivist sociology texts, as the products of human imagination, always carry with them our understanding of the world, of possibility, and of value. Hence, as the author of this text, I am a being with intentions, a narrator of form, and thus every portrayal that I create carries with it my understanding of the world, my understanding of the possibility for transformation, and also my understanding of what has value and what does not. I cannot author texts or create forms that do not *also carry with them my choices* to convey one understanding over another, and I make these choices based on what I deem to be valuable or based on the relations of value that govern my choices. It is possible to alter the formation of social organization based on how we textually portray the world; indeed, social organization has evolved according to our understanding of humanity's relations to the world (Clegg 2009; Gantman 2005; Luke 1993; Smith 1990). We can view all forms of organizational relations—practice—as embodying authorial meaning, which is to say that we can view them as textual relations.

Luke shares Agger's concern with the decline of textuality/contestability in fast capitalism. For Luke (1989a), informational society reduces our realization that "texts are volatile and fragile tissues of codes, kitting together diverse signification fragments charged with mythologies, plural meanings, and many different values" (7). Luke (1989a) analyzes how power functions through the stabilization of meaning, and "approaches political behaviors, social forces, institutional structures, and cultural activities as densely encoded but largely decodable *texts*" (7). Yet, as Luke (1989a) demonstrates in *Screens of Power*, these texts pose two challenges: First, when embedded in media, they are often received as though they are not contestable; however, there also is a tendency for texts to be received as though they *are* contestable choices, when in fact they are merely prepackaged forms of artificial resistance (246). (See Grey and Nickel 2009.) Although he is careful to identify individual struggles to subvert "micrologies of power," Luke (1989a) finds reified "scripts" of "artificial negativity" present in the texts of mass media (101). This analysis can be extended to governing practices, including the encoding of public sociology, civil society, and governance.

Similar to Agger's observation of the presence of the political author in the creation of textual portrayals and Luke's observation of the writers of scripts of power, Smith (1990) reveals the presence of the political individual as the creator of organizational texts. Smith explores our specific encounter with organizational texts within the "relations of rule." Ruling, for Smith (1990), takes place "through an actual experience of reading" and "designates the complex of extra-local relations that provide in contemporary societies a specialization of organization, control, and initiative" (5–6). Like Agger and Luke, Smith understands the text as constituting social relations, and this constitution derives from the way in which "texts speak in the absence of speakers" and derive force from their ability to overcome the inherent contestability of social relations (211). For Smith, organizational texts *mean* and "meaning appears as texts" (210).

Organizational texts, Smith argues, are the externalization of "social consciousness in social practices, objectifying, reasoning, knowledge, memory, decision-making, judgement, evaluation, etc., as properties of social organization or discourse rather than as properties of individuals. They are, of course, accomplished only by individuals" (211). Texts, especially the governing forms that circulate within government organizations and between government organizations and nonprofits that they fund, are the result of individual actors' imaginations. Yet, the duplication and circulation of government texts "render organizing functions increasingly independent of individuals" (Smith 1990, 213). I take from Smith that we ought to contest organizational form(ation)s, including the texts that I analyze in what follows, because they are *the externalization of social consciousness.*

Agger, Luke, and Smith share a substantive critique of textuality and the way in which domination functions through the text without our recognizing it as such. It matters how we *experience* texts—it matters whether we know their authors and know them as such. This is an epistemological point because claims of authorlessness, or objectivity, are based on the assumption that we can know the world objectively without taking a stance on its organization and therefore the assumption that we can produce knowledge and texts apolitically, without intervening in the world (Agger 1989a, b, c; Luke 1993). Although they share a concern about the internalization of texts understood without the realization that they could be rewritten, none of these three authors would have us believe that it is always and indefinitely the case that such understandings prevail. As Luke (1989a) explains, "the text is never fully controlled by its author; instead, it is itself finally 'finished' or 'produced' in its reading by others, inevitably leaving meaning surpluses behind and fulfilling meaning deficits when they arise" (7).

Agger, Luke, and Smith argue for exposing the textual as a political opportunity to intervene in the practice of governing. Building on Agger, Luke, and Smith, I proceed with the assumption that texts are the means by which knowledge and practice are relationally performed. Knowledge, its production, its circulation, and the practices that it facilitates are techniques of governing (Foucault 1980). This is to say, to the extent that the ontological and epistemological claims that intellectuals make about the present are taken for granted as permanent, we are governed (Agger 1989b). Contesting these claims therefore is a starting point for transformation.

The Articulation of Power
Through Practiced Portrayal

At the outset of this book I claimed that ontological declarations, such as divisions of labor and a boundary between the state and civil society, cannot be understood as radical transformations unless they describe a radical transformation of epistemological practice. In Chapter Two I claimed that public sociology has been institutionalized along the lines of the instrumental rationality of governing. In Chapter Three I argued that Burawoy's argument for public sociology was first and primarily an argument for the practice of professional sociology and its encodings, which stabilizes the neoliberal state that he claims to oppose. In Chapter Four I claimed that civil society has been institutionalized along the lines of the requirements of governing. In Chapter Five I claimed that, while ontological claims are powerful governors of imagination, this power functions through epistemological practices that resolve ontological contradictions: Declarations of democratic transformation (ontology) rely on efficiency (an instrumental epistemology) to resolve the contradiction between democratic ideals and disciplinary power. Thus, the transformation of the state contributes to the expansion of instrumental practices of governing rather than to "the radical democratic governance" that it claims to observe.

The burden is therefore upon me to demonstrate that the *practices* transmitted through the institutionalization of public sociology, civil society, and neoliberal/network governance betray the *declaration* that the state has undergone a radically democratic transformation of relations of power. In this chapter I demonstrate how the current practice of governing in the "nongovernmental" or "networked" spaces of "civil society" is not only a case for neoliberalism but is also fundamentally consistent with the practice of power/value prior to these supposed transformations. Building on the textual framework established through the insights of Agger, Luke, and Smith, we can understand this *articulation* of power as being embedded in texts infused with value deriving from what we choose to know and what we therefore claim it is possible to do. These texts are political documents because knowledge and its associated practices involve taking a stance on the world. Textual relations therefore exist in the intersection of knowledge and practice according to encodings of value.

In an organizational landscape governed by the neoliberal state, this generation of knowledge and action revolves around the pursuit of *valued knowledge*—its exchange, its use, and its monitoring. For example, government–NGO partnership "between sectors" to deliver services, also known as governance, is achieved through the transfer of money-for-services. Money is one type of encoded text (Agger 1989a) that carries with it a particular relation of practice and a particular hierarchy of value. Money encodes the practices of counting, evaluation, performance, and exchange value, because money must be monitored and controlled, and, because money is constructed to be scarce, it must be used efficiently. Financial partnership encodes social relations in that some activities and knowledge products have exchange value through the medium of money and others do not (Luke 1999, 2005).

The Comparative Nonprofit Sector Project concurs with the transformation of the state thesis and then observes that the nonprofit sector cannot fully participate in the search for "a 'middle way' between sole reliance on the market and sole reliance on the state" because of a "gross lack of basic information about this sector and how it operates" (Salamon, et al. 1999, 5). Based on this observation, the project establishes the following objectives: "It was to fill this gap in basic knowledge and put the nonprofit sector on the economic map of the world.... Document the scope, structure, financing.... Explain why this sector varies in size from place to place.... Evaluate the impact these organizations are having.... Publicize the existence of this set of institutions and increase public awareness of them.... Build local capacity to carry on this work ..." (Salamon, et al. 1999, 5–6).

Language such as "filling gaps" with "documentation," "evaluation," "publicizing," and "building local capacity" is aimed at demonstrating how the knowledge produced can be instrumentalized toward the goals of governing as these goals are expressed by a government agency or foundation. When one submits a grant application, one is typically asked to demonstrate the objectives of the project, evaluation and outcomes, publication of the results, and especially "building local capacity," which refers to how well the initiatives of the funding agency or foundation will be embedded. Grant writers appeal to grant makers through the incorporation of "key words" that encode research objectives with the initiatives of governing. These words then make their way into project reports and publications as "facts" that conceal that they originate in an attempt to fit knowledge production to the objectives of grant makers, such as the Ford Foundation's (2010) "democratic and accountable government."

In order to establish a basis for its "research contribution," the Center for Civil Society Studies must first concur with contemporary governing imperatives, and therefore it asserts a radical transformation that demands its expertise. In addition to establishing a basis for intervention, Box 6-1 demonstrates how, in spite of recent claims about the transformation of the relationship *between* organizations and between organizations and the public in the supposed shift from government to governance, the dominant mode of power *within* modern organizations in 2010 remains science, control, and

Box 6-1 The Transformation of the State

A major shift has occurred in the operation of the public sector in the United States and other countries over the last five decades. At the heart of this change is the proliferation of new instruments, or tools, of public action—loans, loan guarantees, regulation, contracts, cooperative agreements, reimbursement schemes, tax subsidies, vouchers, insurance, and many more. Moreover, many of these new, or newly expanded, tools have in common a reliance on a host of third parties—such as commercial banks, nonprofit organizations, other levels of government, or for-profit companies—to implement public programs. The adoption of these tools has thus transformed the public sector from a provider to an arranger of services, with profound implications for the nature and content of public management and for democratic governance more generally. Those involved in public administration must consequently learn not only how to operate public agencies, but also the distinctive operating requirements of the different tools, many of which involve complex collaborative relationships with private contractors, regulated industries, nonprofit agencies, and other levels of government. The Center has played a pivotal role in calling attention to this development and producing educational and other materials to promote understanding of it. (CCSS 2010b)

instrumental rationality. It is this instrumental epistemology—embedded in texts—that must become contestable in order for a radical transformation to take place.

As part of its governing research agenda, the Center for Civil Society Studies "seeks to improve understanding and the effective functioning of not-for-profit, philanthropic, or 'civil society' organizations in the United States and throughout the world in order to enhance the contribution these organizations can make to democracy and the quality of human life" (Center for Civil Society Studies 2010a). In order to do this, the Center for Civil Society Studies seeks to transform those organizations that are central to governing in an era of neoliberal network governance into an economic contribution. These projects seek to "put the civil society sector on the economic map of the world" (Salamon 2010). This is simultaneously to recreate civil society in the image of the market. This is demonstrated through the Nonprofit Economic Data Project (Boxes 6-2 and 6-3) (CCSS 2010b) and the International Labor Organization Volunteer Measurement Project (Box 6-4) (CCSS 2010c).

The Nonprofit Economic Data Project is an effort to extract productive exchange-value knowledge out of the previously "valueless" realm of social problems and public sentiment; it aims to transform every instance of basic humanity into a countable and productive piece of knowledge dedicated to the stabilization of nonprofit "industries."

Box 6-2 Portraying the Nonprofitable as an Economic Input

The Johns Hopkins Nonprofit Economic Data Project is generating critical new information on the dynamics of the nonprofit sector. As such, it is reshaping how this important sector is viewed in local, state, and regional economies and providing cutting-edge insights into the key trends affecting the various nonprofit industries such as nursing homes, hospitals, home health centers, education, social services, and the arts.... A collaboration between the Center for Civil Society Studies, state employment security agencies, the U.S. Bureau of Labor Statistics, and state nonprofit associations, the NED Project is yielding a vital resource for understanding the nonprofit sector.... The new *Nonprofit Economic Data Project* has created a capability to offer the most up-to-date, in-depth analyses available of the nonprofit sector and its component parts at the national, regional, state, or local level. (CCSS 2010c)

The project clearly states that its goal is to reshape the sector in the image of profitability and instrumentality, what Horkheimer and Adorno (1989, 4) called the "factual mentality." Nonprofits are stripped of their transformational potential by the project text as they are measured factually according to their potential to "yield" labor and economic growth. The project celebrates its ability to eliminate any distinguishing characteristics of nonproductive "third sector" knowledge from economically productive knowledge, dissolving the boundary by which the nonprofit sector could represent possibilities other than the market and its associated texts. The project takes a stance on social organization as it asserts that all *nonmeasurable labor* is valueless; in order to achieve value, our humanity must be measured according to what it contributes to the economy. "Nonprofit impact" is unbelievably framed solely in terms of wages, employment, and economic contribution of volunteers.

The idea of human well-being is, disturbingly, nowhere present in these governing documents. The data instruments employed by the project are not only instrumental, but disciplinary tools born of instrumental rationality— "timetables, collective training, exercises, total and detailed surveillance, perpetual assessment and classification" (Foucault 1995). Such "expertly derived data" practices divorce the nonexpert public from the third sector by valuing the highly professionalized practice of the Center for Civil Society Studies over the nonprofessionalized knowledge of the public. Conflict over knowledge is thus truncated by expertise and "official knowledge" (Agger 1989c; Apple 1993, 2003).

It is true, as Box 6-3 argues, that "the data source we have tapped to examine this facet of nonprofit operations is extremely powerful." As Smith (1990) argues of government documents, the ES-202 and IRS Form 990 are subjective and powerful practices, not objects/texts (214). Our objective if we are to *radicalize* power is to make these "documents or texts visible

> **Box 6-3 Portraying Civil Society as Wages, Employment, and Economic Contribution**
>
> ---
>
> Our Center works with clients across the country to develop reports documenting the important economic role of nonprofits in localities, states and regions, or in specific industries such as the arts, social services, healthcare, and education. Our research generally examines three important measures of nonprofit impact: 1) Wages and employment 2) Nonprofit finances 3) Volunteering
>
> ### Wages and Employment
>
> Employment is an extraordinarily useful indicator of the economic activity of nonprofit organizations since these organizations are known to be highly "labor-intensive." What is more, the data source we have tapped to examine this facet of nonprofit operations is extremely powerful. This data source is the so-called ES-202 data program operated by state Labor Market Information (LMI) offices in cooperation with the U.S. Bureau of Labor Statistics. Designed to collect official information for the nation's Unemployment Insurance program, the ES-202 data system also serves as an exciting new resource for understanding the scope and dynamics of nonprofit activity both locally and nationally....
>
> Despite its advantages, the ES-202 data have historically not been available to yield information on the nonprofit sector.... Working with state LMI officials, state nonprofit associations, and the federal Bureau of Labor Statistics, we have now found ways to tap into the ES-202 data source and extract data on nonprofit places of employment. The result has been to unlock a treasure trove of timely information on the scope, structure, and changing fortunes on the nonprofit sector in states and regions throughout the country....
>
> ### Nonprofit Finances
>
> By tapping into data from the IRS Form 990, which is required of all nonprofits with expenditures in excess of $25,000, we are able to measure the financial scope of nonprofit organizations nationally and in different states and regions....
>
> ### Volunteering
>
> An important, yet often overlooked, nonprofit resource is the contribution of volunteers. By tapping into Census Bureau surveys of volunteer work, we can estimate the economic contribution of volunteer workers to their local, state or region's economy, and further detail the sector's significant strength and human capital resources.... (CCSS 2010c)

as constituents of social relations ... the appearance of meaning as a text, that is, in a permanent material form, detaches meaning from the lived processes of its transitory construction, made and remade at each moment of people's talk" (Smith 1990, 210). The employment of organizational texts such as IRS Form 990 and ES-202 data makes the uniformity of organizational texts seem unproblematic, when in fact these texts encode the state and its imposition of instrumentality upon what is framed as a "civil society" project, a form of instrumental rationality manifested as a relation of domination (Horkheimer and Adorno 1989), which the highly professionalized constitution of the sector and its experts depoliticize through an appeal to expertise within which it seems that we *cannot mediate* (Horkheimer and Adorno 1989; Agger 1989a, 1989b, 1989c). The International Labor Organization Volunteer Measurement Project further collapses the boundary between the state knowledge, profit, and social action, as it produces a manual for how "global civil society" will be governed according to technical expertise. "Valuing citizens" in this case does not mean caring for citizens as human beings, it means reducing them to a discrete economic value. It is unclear how counting "civil society" and making it into the image of labor will contribute anything to human well-being, or even to politics. The suggestion that a technical manual for counting "hours worked" and "value added" by volunteers will have even a negligible positive impact on anything

---

Box 6-4 Transforming Volunteer Work into a Portrayal of Labor

**The Johns Hopkins University/International Labour Organization
Volunteer Measurement Project**

What efforts have been made to measure volunteer work have been sporadic and frequently uncoordinated, leaving us without up-to-date, reliable data on the scope of this important social and economic phenomenon. With these facts in mind, the UN General Assembly passed a resolution in 2001 calling on member governments to "enhance the knowledge base" on volunteering and to support efforts to "measure" its contributions.... In April 2007, the International Labour Organization (ILO) and the Johns Hopkins Center for Civil Society Studies entered into a Memorandum of Understanding under which ILO authorized JHU/CCSS to produce a draft of an ILO *Manual on the Measurement of Volunteer Work* through official labour force surveys and a draft Volunteer Measurement Survey Module.... The proposed ILO *Manual on the Measurement of Volunteer Work* will make available a standardized mechanism for generating the comparative data needed to comply with this mandate through a regular supplement to existing labour force surveys. If adopted by the ICLS and implemented in countries, this will revolutionize the information available about the work of volunteers and help boost the visibility and credibility of volunteer work throughout the world.... (CCSS 2010d)

other than the authority of the counters themselves is baseless. Indeed, my argument is that it has a negative impact on the exercise of political agency, because it imposes expertise on the process of living together. *Counting matters and it matters powerfully.* The valuation advanced by the Johns Hopkins University/International Labour Organization Volunteer Measurement Project creates a hierarchy of the "valued over the valueless" (Agger 1993), *devaluing anything that cannot be counted as a contribution to economic growth.* This is not the empowerment of "civil society" or a radical transformation of power; it is the *disempowerment of anything that does not contribute to economic growth.* As Agger (1989a) explains: "Fast capitalism reproduces itself through this circuitry between the realms of valued and valueless activity—work and home, public and private, men and women, science and fiction, practice and theory. The domination of reproduction, degraded into mere intellection, text, superstructure, reproduces domination by providing a reserve army of labor and unpaid houseworkers through which a capitalist lifeworld perpetuates itself" (60–61).

Organizational texts, including the incentives for particular texts to be produced by organizations within network governance partnerships, conceal value and hierarchy in a sort of epistemological political economy. As Agger (1989b) notes, these figures encode "the hierarchical social relations that brought them about in the first place" (89). This is to say, the Center for Civil Society Studies texts involve value decisions that were made in the process of their construction. Agger's point is that these figures, by virtue of being authored, are political statements open to alternative interpretations; they can be written otherwise, and thus we always have a starting point for living according to a different set of rules—other forms of organization are possible, and our construction of alternatives to the present is valuable. The Center for Civil Society Studies projects, especially in their emphasis on labor and wages, are texts that evolved as a result of oppressive social relations, but falsely portray themselves as being "facts rather than literary acts" (Agger 2000). It is a false portrayal that impedes transformation, because we do not recognize that these hierarchical social relations of value are not matters of fact, but matters of choice. The hierarchy that we ought to be focused on transforming is not a chain of command, but the hierarchy of value, in which that which is not measurable is subjugated to that which is. Smith (1990) helps us to extend this insight to networked organizations when she notes that: "Information, knowledge, reasoning, decision making, control, etc., become properties of external organizational and technological forms. They are accomplished in a division of labor concerted discursively or hierarchically. The social relations of textually mediated discourse intersect and penetrate organizational structures constituted as complex entities with differentiated functions, corporations, government agencies, universities, and so on" (8). The seepage of production values into supposedly noninstrumental texts via organizations in an era of neoliberal network governance is "the fusion of two disparate and allegedly antithetical material logics—the academic/scholarly and the capitalist/professionalistic—into an elaborate disciplinary system of knowledge production and producer valorization" (Luke 1999, 349).

Extending Luke's analysis of performativity from the university as an organization to other "noncapitalist" forms of organization, we can say the same of all organizations that are transformed into sites of production to the extent that that they take on productive texts and attempt to resolve the voluntary/civic with the capitalist/professionalistic. This is especially true as "criteria borrowed from the real worlds of exchange-value are now imposed upon the use-value regions" (Luke 1999, 349–350), which include not only the areas of teaching and research with which Luke is concerned, but also the inherent value of transformative public sentiment, now disparagingly valorized and referred to as "social capital" that produces efficient policies. It is these criteria, specifically the criterion that knowledge be produced for exchange-value rather than transformative-value, that marginalizes and subjugates the formation of knowledge that would be the basis for transformation. This is precisely Agger's point when he argues that texts encode hierarchy: Authorial choices must be made in order for organizational texts to be written and proceed to govern (1989a, b). The problem is therefore not only the way in which value is assigned, but also the means by which this value is deemed to be inherent rather than a matter of authorial choice.

My argument, following Agger, Luke, and Smith, is that anti-textual calculability as it is preached by the Center for Civil Society Studies is now encoded so deeply in organizational epistemology in every sector and stabilized so firmly by the logics of "public sociology from the standpoint of civil society" and "radically democratic network governance" that we fail to recognize them as political, and thus we fail to transform practice. Whether or not we have shifted from hierarchal government to network governance, *neoliberalism and its associated epistemological relations of value remain the shared text of most social organization.* Network governance has not transformed textual practice, but has rather increased belief in the supposed inevitability of instrumentality and control as these practices have been transferred from the market and the state into "civil society," through the blurring of boundaries of practice and value. The notion of a shifting organizational landscape misdirects our political imagination away from the actual space of ruling. Ruling takes place in the intersection of knowledge and practice, and thus it is in this space where transformation must take place.

The transformation of the state thesis and its proffering of democratic network governance coalesce with neoliberal constructions of value in a difficult-to-discern epistemological confluence that is stabilized by the politics from which knowledge about the network is derived and the texts through which it is practiced. The transfer between sectors through neoliberal network governance of money and other texts, such as the author-generated questions resulting in the data sets used by the NEDP, allows for the seamless transfer of practices and associated hierarchies of value from one sector to another under the guise of supposedly neutral texts and their encoded practices. It is therefore problematic to begin with governing partnerships based on the categories of "relatively autonomous actors" (Sørensen and Torfing 2005a, b), including for-profit organization, nonprofit organization, and governmental organization as a starting point for analysis. The problem is that, despite the distinction made regarding profit, all of these labels describe organizations that employ encoded relations of practice and value; whether they are producing a surplus or not, most mainstream modern organizations practice the same relations through texts such as money and data.

A radical democratic transformation of the state would start with a radical democratization of the relationship between epistemology and value as they are embedded in texts and their portrayal of possibility. We are no closer to such a transformation in "an era of network governance" than we were at the height of scientific management. As Ernest Mandel (1992) noted, "we must make a careful distinction between power relations and the devolution of power on the one hand, and the *articulation of power* involving specialized knowledge on the other hand" (228). The use of adjectives does not guarantee anything about the nouns that they modify and, as I demonstrate further in Chapter Seven, in the case of "public sociology," "global civil society," and "the radical transformation of the state," there currently is little opportunity to contest the *decisions about knowledge* upon which the current practice of collective action is based.

When the language that governs our lives is not our own, instead emerging from a space of assumed meaning not originating from our lived experience in the world, governing is distanced from the lives that it claims to seek to enhance through collective action. It therefore matters whether or not the texts that portray social organization, including the transformation of the state thesis, are openly discursive in the sense that we could argue on behalf of alternative meanings in response their encodings. The articulation of power—*practice*—cannot be transformative until we recognize that the basis for transformation is not the shifting constellation of organizations; rather, it is the political economy of the practice of *textual knowledge* according to which such shifting organizational constellations govern.

Chapter 7

NGOs, the State, and Governance as Rites of Rule

Advocates of public sociology have much to say about human rights, but say curiously little about the power/knowledge relationship in which they are embedded. Burawoy's (2006) campaign in the edited volume *Public Sociologies Reader* in favor of "a public sociology for human rights," conducted with his interlocutors as a narrative of cosmopolitan global governance, places an emphasis on the intersection between public sociology, human rights, nongovernmental organizations (NGOs), the state, and professionalized knowledge (Beck 2005b; Burawoy 2006; Delanty 2006; Pubantz and Moore Jr. 2006; Ugalde and Homedes 2006). However, absent from this crusade is recognition of how this regime governs through the transfer of productive knowledge. Public sociology for human rights, as it is conceived by Burawoy, fails to problematize the cosmopolitan human rights regime, which, in practice, often is an authoritarian and hierarchical regime of power, where power is conceived of as the manifestation of the practice of instrumental knowledge (Horkheimer and Adorno 1989; Foucault 1980, 1991, 1995, 2002).

In this chapter I argue that the "rites of rule" (Luke 1996) imposed by the regime of knowledge, right(s), and the state-NGO-knowledge-rite regime advocated by Burawoy stabilizes the present as a rite of passage according to the narrative of development. My argument is structured in four parts. First, I begin by demonstrating how the narrative of public sociology for human rights stabilizes unquestioningly the legitimacy of cosmopolitan global governance. Second, I argue that, although admirable in its stated aim, this framing of public sociology for human rights neglects to reveal its roots in governmentality and thus does not recognize the empirical practice of human rights as consolidated contragovernmentality, which in turn facilitates the legitimacy of the development. Third, I demonstrate that public sociology's participation in the human rights regime, as it is advocated by Burawoy, conflates human rights and market rights through the narrative of development as a rite of passage. Finally, I demonstrate how public sociology for human rights stabilizes the practice of human rights as rites of rule, which subjugates rights (entitlement) to right (correct) in an attempt to stabilize a new logic of ruling.

"Public Sociology for Human Rights" as Cosmopolitan Global Governance

I fully support the ideal of universal human well-being. It is for this reason that I am critical of the practice of public sociology for human rights, because it is currently framed as cosmopolitan global governance, which is, in practice, a regime often dedicated to universal development/exploitation, as though profit and environmental degradation are the source rather than the denial of human well-being. Public sociology for human rights is first expressed by Burawoy (2006) in the introduction to *Public Sociologies Reader.* Citing the aftermath of Hurricane Katrina and civil wars in Sudan, Rwanda, Afghanistan, Bosnia, and Herzegovina, Burawoy (2006) correctly points out that the world is full of atrocities; he then points out that "the advantage of a human rights framework is its widespread appeal. Who, after all, can be against human rights?" (5).

Burawoy is correct that human rights are highly marketable, no less for sociology than for Angelina Jolie, Bono, Coca-Cola, Starbucks, and Oprah Winfrey. Although no doubt there are genuine humanitarianisms and genuine humanitarians concerned with human rights, and Burawoy is correct that they are appealing, there are also commodified and exploitative humanitarianisms that impose on everyday practice the very ontological and epistemological frameworks that are the basis for the *denial* of human rights.[1] It is not the ideal of human rights as human well-being that needs evaluation, but the way in which human rights are practically situated as rites, or those rituals and practices that stabilize the necessity of the present. Like truth, rights are "a thing of this world" (Foucault 1980, 131).

The theme of public sociology for human rights is buttressed in the *Public Sociologies Reader* by cosmopolitanism, as it is articulated by Beck (2005a, b) and Delanty (2006) in their discussions of public sociology. Delanty argues that cosmopolitanism, a form of governance, is "essential to public sociology" (Delanty 2006, 38). Beck (2005b) argues that public sociology is in "danger of *reaching false conclusions from nation-state premises*" (340), which is an extension of his (2005a) call for a new cosmopolitan realism, which shares its ontology with the market: "The counter-power of global civil society is based on the figure of the *political consumer* ... not buying certain products and therefore casting a vote against the politics of corporations ... is completely free of risk" (7). When considering Burawoy's public sociology for human rights, we are thus involved in the legitimation of the so-called shift from government to governance; from the nation-state as the locus of legitimate power to networks of non-state actors as the locus of legitimate power. As I explained in Chapter Three, Burawoy's (2006) introduction to "a public sociology for human rights" asserts a fictional distinction between the state, the market, and civil society, holding the state and the market responsible for the advance of neoliberalism, while absolving sociology of any epistemological stabilization, because it supposedly belongs exclusively to civil society and keeps its distance from the state and the market (8).[2] Burawoy has made a false distinction among the state, civil society, and the market, while simultaneously calling for cosmopolitan global governance, which collapses these distinctions altogether.

"A public sociology for human rights," as Burawoy (2006) has framed it, is a public sociology practiced through nongovernmental organizations (NGOs) and other voluntary associations, which he refers to as collective self organizations (9). Of course, as I argued in Chapters Four and Five, NGOs are not at all distinct from the state and the market, but often are dependent on both for funding and legitimacy, if they are not completely co-opted, as time once spent with human beings in need is increasingly spent with accountability forms and training in the *means of right* (Chandhoke 2003; Hayden 2002; Kamat 2003; INCITE! 2007). Describing civil society as "Janus-faced," Burawoy (2006) notes such limitations—"[NGOs] become the lubricant and contraceptive of third-wave marketization. Global civil society is Janus-faced—decisively shaped by and connected to the interests of nation-states and multilateral agencies even as it is also terrain for contesting those interests" (10). In spite of his recognition of the limitations of the supposedly lubricating tendencies of civil society, Burawoy continued to argue for a public sociology from the standpoint of civil society. As I discussed in Chapter Four, civil society is constituted by the state and sovereignty and thus the idea of public sociology from the standpoint of civil society is already an argument on behalf of the state.

To clarify, then, Burawoy is arguing for a public sociology for human rights operating from the standpoint of civil society, a space that he frames as being distinct from the state and the market and the unique purview of sociology, which is, in contraction to his previous (2005a) division of labor for sociology, theorized as being independent from and in opposition to the state (and thus, we might assume, in opposition to his professional and policy sociologists). As I mentioned in Chapter Two, the periodization by which Burawoy (2006) discusses the state, market, and neoliberalism is derived from Polanyi's (1944) *The Great Transformation,* or commodification. Based on his reading of Polanyi, Burawoy names the present period "third wave marketization." A closer reading of Polanyi would reveal that commodification and transformation are, at the least, partially the result of the politics of knowing; yet, Burawoy offers no explanation of power and epistemology in relationship to the state or the market.

In his introduction to a "public sociology for human rights" in opposition to the state and the market Burawoy (2007c) argues that "Sociology lives and dies with society. When society is threatened so is sociology. We can no longer rely on the state to contain the market and so sociologists have to forge their own connections to society, i.e. to develop public sociology. We have to do more than passively serve society, but have to conserve and constitute society" (366). Of course, sociology does not live and die with society; it frequently lives and dies with the state (Gouldner 1970), and when the state devolves more governing functions to civil society, as it has done in the supposed shift from "government to governance," then sociology typically follows in order to stay "legitimate" and maybe even edge political science and economics out of the monopoly over the governing game. "Conserving and constituting society" is, of course, a governing activity dating back to Comte's positivism and is by no means automatically a democratic one; fascists also conserved and constituted society, and thus it would seem that sociology is at least equally as guilty as "the economists and political scientists." Burawoy (2006) then claims the territory known as "civil society," which, he argues is best governed by sociology as the saviour/*savoir.* As I demonstrated in Chapter Four, nation-states have been reasserting civil society as the best possible space from which to govern since circa 1988; in his call for governing from the standpoint of civil society Burawoy is at least fifteen years behind the neoliberal brigade. Framing civil society as the sole space within which to achieve well-being fortifies the neoliberal state as it absorbs the supposedly bloated bureaucracy into its aura of democracy so that the state might appear leaner and more market-like in the interest of making the market and its anemic rituals seem more robustly legitimate (see Luke 1990).

Despite this argument for a cosmopolitan public sociology in which *sociology governs through civil society* more legitimately than do the state and the market, Burawoy does not offer an explicit theory of the state, except to reject the category of nation-state in favor of cosmopolitanism. The argument in general for public sociology as cosmopolitanism, drawing on Beck (2005a, 2005b), Delanty (2006), and Burawoy (2006), is that the state is now what Beck (2005a) calls a "zombie category," and thus we need a "new realism" beyond the nation-state. However, public sociology for a cosmopolitanism regime of human rights merely replaces sovereignty as the study of power with human rights as the study of power, still neglecting the "techniques and tactics of domination" (Foucault 1980, 102).

Although it is a critical ideal, there is nothing particularly revolutionary about the contemporary practice of cosmopolitanism. Although it claims to rejecting the nation-state, in practice, this stance still favors analysis of the juridicial and institutional over analysis of the practice of domination through the rituals of rights. Given Gouldner's (1970) observation that the growth of sociology was dependent on the welfare state, it is not at all surprising to now learn that public sociology is dependent on the growth of global cosmopolitan governance. The adaptability of sociology to the needs of state does not ensure human well-being and neither does the adaptability of sociology to the needs of global capital and its mythology of development. Although he claims to be critical of neoliberalism, Burawoy's stance is based in an affirmative theory of the state/governance that neglects the way in which knowledge functions to discipline human rights in concert with neoliberalism (Harvey 2005, 2006). Human rights, as we will see, are conflated with neoliberalism's view of human rights as development rights—a view as old as the Enlightenment (Horkheimer and Adorno 1989).

From Governmentality to Consolidated Contragovernmentality

The rise of cosmopolitan governance, network governance, global governance, and the general narrative of the supposedly radical transformation upon which the human rights regime is practiced is old news. The state has been "unbundling" for decades (Luke 1990, 1996, 2007). The idea that such an unbundling is in the service of human rights is certainly functional, but it is hardly transformative. In order to understand how public sociology for human rights as Burawoy has framed it can only result in the further subjugation of human rights to instrumentality, we first need to shift the discussion of public sociology in relationship to the state and rights from Burawoy's conceptual categories, which are based in acceptance of the myth of the boundary between the state, market, and civil society and the legitimacy of public sociology governing within a global cosmopolitan realism.

Pace Burawoy, my stance on rights does not begin with a boundary between the state, the market, and civil society and an equivalent boundary between political science, economics, and sociology. I begin from an alternative starting point in governmentality (Foucault 1991) and the shift to what Luke (1996) has called contragovernmentality. In other words, I argue that the shift in the practice of the state on rights was not from sovereignty to cosmopolitanism or from the welfare state to neoliberalism or even from government to governance; the shift was from governmentality to contragovernmentality. From the perspective of governmentality, public sociology for human rights is governmentalized as the practice of human rights.

To begin with, governmentality, as Foucault (1991) originally theorized it, involved:

> The ensemble formed by the institutions, procedures, analyses and reflections, the calculations and tactics that allow the exercise of this very specific albeit complex form of power, which has as its target population, as its principal form of knowledge [—] political economy, and its essential technical means [—] apparatuses of security … [which] steadily led towards the pre-eminence over all other forms (sovereignty, discipline, etc.) of this type of power which may be termed government, resulting, on the one hand, in the formation of a whole series of specific governmental apparatuses, and on the other, in the development of a whole complex of *savoirs*. (102–103)

Governmentality is instructive in the case of the supposed shift from *sovereignty*-in-relationship-to-the-state to *human-rights*-in-relationship-to-global-civil-society because, according to Foucault (1991), the modern practice of government never involved only sovereignty, but was a "triangle, sovereignty-discipline-government" (102). The focus on human rights as the basis for a public sociology opposed to the nation-state/market thus neglects at least two angles of the triangle through which the management of the population is achieved.

In an era of cosmopolitan global governance, this triangle of sovereignty-discipline-government gives way to human rights-discipline-governance, through the consolidation of what Luke (1996) named contragovernmentality. Contragovernmentality involved "decentered sovrans," which became institutionalized as the very NGOs and collective organizations to which Burawoy (2006) assigns the right to rule through the right *rites*—the ritual practices, techniques, and knowledges involved in governing. These rites to manage the population have not changed; only the logic in the shift from sovereignty to rights as the basis of rule and the shift from government to governance as the territory of the apparatus through which techniques and knowledge are practiced has changed. Luke (1996) explains that:

> Contragovernmentality rewrights people as many different kinds of denationalized agents—believer, viewer, consumer, listener, gendered, racialized, reclassed, dialected, faithful, truthful, skillful, watchful—operating in new cultural and economic domains written against the state by non-statal forces. Power, conflict, and struggle continue, but more often now at very amodernized sites, which are becoming de-territorialized, un-stated, contra-governmental spaces. (492)

In its 1996 context, contragovernmentality involved the dislocation of national governmentalities as strategies of "dissolution of territoriality and degradation of sovereignty" (493). However, this dissolution has now been reordered through the transfer of rites and consolidated through the logic of cosmopolitanism, by which denationalization is consolidated through a process that Luke (1990), with Paul Piccone (1978), earlier theorized as artificial negativity:

> Counter-bureaucratic bureaucracies become one of the paradoxical expressions of artificially generated negativity. The problem with this system-generated negativity is that, to the extent that it is itself bureaucratically sanctioned, it tends to become an extension of the very bureaucracy in need of control … it simply extends the bureaucratic logic it was meant to challenge and becomes counter-productive. The organic negativity necessary to successfully sustain this challenge must develop outside the bureaucratic administrative framework. (Piccone 1978, 48)

By 2006, when Burawoy argues for public sociology for human rights, the origins of contragovernmentality have transformed from what might have originally been formations of organic resistance in 1996 as they have become bureaucratically sanctioned and consolidated within cosmopolitan governance, often through grant funding by national governments and the *sovran*ty of sociological knowledge.

Contragovernmentality, as theorized by Luke (1996), like governmentality, involves a complex of practices and knowledge, but, where legitimacy was once assigned to government, it is now assigned to actors who have been legitimated within cosmopolitan global governance. Consolidated contragovernmentality shares with cosmopolitanism the observation that sovereignty has been degraded as a legitimating idea; where sovereignty was once the locus of "legitimate" power, the authority of government action, now human rights are the locus of "legitimate" cosmopolitan power and governance as action. "Extra-legitimate" power through rites, however, is not taken into account in either legitimating logic, both of which serve the same function: to forestall resistance to discipline through the stabilization of practice. This shift therefore is not reason for uncritical celebration of a supposedly grand democratic transfer of rule from the nation-state to global civil society, because rule always took place through rite and rite is still an "ensemble formed by the institutions, procedures, analyses and reflections, the calculations and tactics that allow the exercise of this very specific albeit complex form of power, which has as its target population, as its principal form of knowledge political economy, and its essential technical means apparatuses of security"(Foucault 1991, 102).

To the extent that, as with the rise of governmentality, consolidated contragovernmentality achieves "security, territory, and population" as truth production becomes institutionalized as techniques of practice (rites), what we have witnessed is the shift from sovereignty to human rights as a source of legitimation and a shift from government to governance as a locus of practice. The ensemble of governmentality might have been disengaged from the legitimacy of sovereignty, but the ensemble of contragovernmentality practiced through governance rather than government does not abandon the objective of power through knowledge (right) and apparatuses of security (rite). Liberal government-for-the-sovereign and cosmopolitan-governance-for-human-rights are both a means of ensuring "the emergence of population as datum, as a field of intervention and as an objective of governmental techniques, and the process which isolates the economy as a specific sector of reality" (Foucault 1991, 102). The objective of the rites of rule has not changed, and neither have the techniques; only the population, which is now cosmopolitan; the economy, which is global and also an object of development; and the legitimating logic, which is now human rights.

Contragovernmentality, in this conception (Figure 7-1), territorializes based not on sovereignty, but on human rights. Government shifts to governance, the techniques of rule now fully legitimated in their panoptical formation (Foucault 1995). Human rights work becomes "economically advantageous" (Foucault 1980, 101), and thus knowledge services the production of the practices of rite (modernity's rituals of practice) on rights (entitlements) by those organizations that are right (correct) about human rights as they are determined by those who have the means to fund and discursively construct human rights practice. As with madness, human rights "lend themselves to economic profit … as a natural consequence, all of a sudden, they became colonised and maintained by global mechanisms and the entire State system" (Foucault 1980, 101). Human rights are useful for

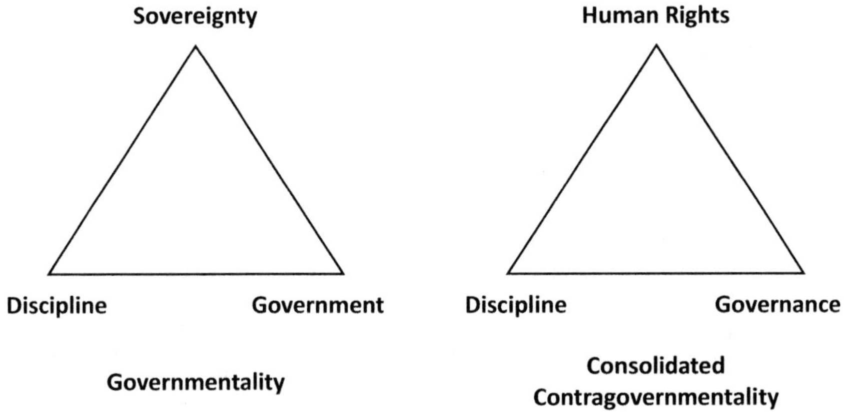

Figure 7-1 The Shift from Governmentality to Consolidated Contragovernmentality

development because they provide a legitimating logic, a basis of intervention, for the exercise of power over "undeveloped" territories, or territories that are still difficult for global capital to exploit. At its worst, the regime of rite ruling human rights is not interested in human well-being any more than the nineteenth-century bourgeoisie was interested in madness: The regime of rite is interested in control and thus exercises discipline through human rights. Human rights are brought into line as instrumental rites, and, since the advent of Enlightenment, it has been these rites that ruled, regardless of the logic of rule.

Consolidated Contragovernmental Rites of Passage: The Conflation of Right(s) and Development

That human rights are increasingly conflated with development and its associated rites can be observed as the ideals of world peace and human rights are increasingly embedded in development-speak (see Hilhorst 2003). In 2006 the Nobel Peace Prize was awarded to economist Muhammad Yunus of Bangladesh. The United Nations News Service reported that "speaking at UN Headquarters in New York during a tribute to Professor Yunus, who founded the Grameen Bank, Mr. Malloch Brown hailed the Bangladeshi as a banker, advocate, activist and champion for the poor. 'You have done wonderful things for development and by doing that you have done wonderful things for peace', he told the laureate" (UN News Centre 2006). In a similar construction of development as peace, General Assembly President Sheikha Haya Al Khalifa was quoted as saying that "the Grameen Bank has disbursed over $5 billion in micro-credit loans to 7 million borrowers, 97 percent of whom are women, thus making 'a tremendous contribution towards ending poverty in Bangladesh'" (UN News Centre 2006). Within this narrative, loans are equated with the elimination of poverty and world peace. This is problematic because Professor Yunus has not donated $5 billion; he has created a debt of $5 billion, which could also be understood as potentially increasing poverty. Debt is only inaccurately equated with dignity. For the UN and the Norwegian Nobel Committee, creating a $5 billion debt is equated with creating world peace. According to this logic, Visa, MasterCard, and predatory lending agencies are also agents of world peace. World peace becomes predicated on banking; so deeply held is this belief that capitalist finance is the only means to achieve world peace that the Nobel Peace Prize is awarded to a banker who created a new market for the creation of debt, "[disabling] men even as it nurtures them" (Horkheimer and Adorno 1989, 37).

If human rights are achieved through development, then all social action can only be justly and humanely oriented toward the market, and thus is it possible for a banker to be awarded the Nobel Peace Prize for creating debt.

Hugo Slim (2003), chief scholar for the Centre for Humanitarian Dialogue in Switzerland, argues that the distinction between humanitarianism and development ought to be dissolved completely:

> That dreadful tendency to dualism which dogs the Western mind and has led to the pernicious idea that humanitarianism and development are different pursuits.... It is in human rights that we can finally dissolve the unhelpful dualism between humanitarianism and development.... If, in the new century, humanitarians and development workers could both take the bold step of recognising that they are all human-rights workers, then, the theory, management, and practice of relief and development work would be relieved of one of their most mesmerizing and exhausting distractions—the false dichotomy between these two professions and their common values. (22–25)

Slim is correct that development and humanitarianism are often the same practice; however, this is not to the advantage of human well-being. The ideal, as Slim has presented it, of conflating development and human rights is distinctly problematic because it assumes that development is the only possible path toward human rights, thus tying human rights to the market and commodifiying well-being. Slim's call for dissolving the supposed "false dichotomy" between the rights of humans and the right of development is a call for development rights as human rights—the practice of human rights as development rites. When rights cannot be distinguished from development it follows that rights can only be achieved *through* development.

If development and human rights are functionally the same, or even if they are "only" narratively the same, is it important for those who genuinely are concerned with human well-being to understand what development is in practice. For Mitchell (2002), development "is a discourse of rational planning. To plan effectively, it must grasp the object of its planning in its entirety. It must represent on the plans it draws up every significant aspect of the reality with which it is dealing..." (233). This is so, argues Mitchell (2002), because the foundations upon which development bases the legitimacy of its actions—democracy and pluralism—are untrue in practice. For Mitchell (2002), Slim's "theory, management, and practice of relief and development work" *makes* human rights through the practice of experts, who create binaries with human expertise on one side and nature on the other (35).

As an objective of development, human rights become valorized as development *inputs* and "economized as a site of production" imposing a "hierarchy of value over the devalued" (Agger 1993, 121). It is not true that development is equivalent to the achievement of human rights unless human rights are (falsely) conceived of as being market rights achieved through market rites, a logic that results in domination of the valueless by the valued (Agger 1993). Development is completely barren of a normative basis independent of the market. This is so because human well-being can be and has for eons been achieved independently of the new global hypermarket. Development attempts to achieve universal participation in global capitalism in order to protect global capitalism from the risk of collapse as a result of nonparticipation. The ethically barren discourse of development, which is simply preparation for the rite of passage to market participation, therefore *needs* the discourse of human rights, now provided by public sociology, in order to justify its emphasis on economic engineering. The conflation of rights and development overcomes neoliberalism's need for a normative rationality. While Jurgen Habermas (1971) was troubled that "the leading productive force—controlled scientific-technical progress itself—has now become the basis of legitimation" (111), the conflation of human rights and development brings the leading productive force to the forefront by rewriting the productive force as a normative force on behalf of human rights. The aforementioned logic of debt as peace is a case in point.

It is not only economists and development scientists who argue on behalf of the market as the basis for human rights. Burawoy (2006) himself tacitly supports development and the market as the basis for human rights, even as he argues that sociology must defend human rights against the market. In his discussion of the introduction of public sociology at the ASA meetings, Burawoy (2005b) writes, "On the second evening [of the ASA meetings] Mary Robinson, former President of Ireland, former UN High Commissioner for Human Rights, spoke of the close connection between human rights work and public sociology . . ." (418). Yet, in *Human Rights and Development: Towards Mutual Reinforcement* Mary Robinson with Philip Alston specifically argued for human rights to be practiced *as* development (Alston and Robinson 2005), and thus her support of a public sociology for human rights against the market concerns me as a defense of public sociology. Robinson and Alston argue that human rights must be *mainstreamed* in concert with development, thus completely collapsing the space between human rights and the market that Burawoy proposes that we must defend them against.

It is problematic that the human rights regime of rite governs not on behalf of human rights, but through development as human rights/rites, which frames compliance with human rights and their associated rituals of rite as a rite of passage to the "developed world." The practice of human rights typically shares its rites with development, which, because it belongs to the same ontological and funding regimes, in turn is the practice of market rites, which is the practice of subjugating rights to the market through the construction of the right to participate in the market rightly. Such rites neglect that commodification of well-being is a denial of human rights, because it forces individuals into market participation for survival. We therefore cannot predicate human rights, as a resistance to commodification, on development, which is itself commodification. Development is instrumentality and its management practices achieved through the dominance of rites over rights.

In order to demonstrate how knowledge subjugates rights to right, next I examine those practices exercised as the defense of human rights—the domination of rights by right—as they are manifest and enforced by the congregation that officiates the rite of passage from predevelopment to development, the United Nations Office of the High Commissioner for Human Rights (OHCHR), a body that is endorsed by Burawoy (2005b) *as* public sociology.

The Practice of Human Rights as Rites of Rule

Advocates of public sociology for human rights appear to be rather naive about the *practice* of being "for human rights." Human rights are currently framed within the language of global capitalism and are not practiced as the right to well-being, but as development and its associated "rites of rule" (Luke 1996). The human rights regime of rite—the nation-state, global capital, NGOs, IGOs, and the academics charged with the legitimation of performative knowledges (Lyotard 1984)—is charged with the creation of meaning and subsequently the employment and monitoring of meaning. In opposition to this regime of rite, which governs human rights, our second task in regard to human rights is to reveal how their obfuscation is achieved through epistemological hierarchy, which is embedded in the practices and institutions of the rights regime and its creation of rites of passage (see van Gennep 1909). As Foucault (1991) observed: "it is the tactics of government which make possible the continual definition and redefinition of what is within the competence of the state and what is not, the public versus the private, and so on; the state can only be understood in its survival and its limits on the basis of the general tactics of governmentality" (Foucault 1991, 103). I view these tactics as the rites and the rituals of marketized modernity, to which the development discourse belongs (Mitchell 2002). As exercised by the regime of rites—including NGOs, the states that fund them, and the academics who advocate their right to rule—human rights are practiced *as* the tactics of consolidating contragovernmentality, or governmentality according to the shift from sovereignty to human rights as a legitimating logic.

The human rights regime often stabilizes through rites the very ontological realisms and epistemological frameworks that are the basis for the *denial* of human rights. How we endeavor to know a particular version of the world *properly* in turn functions politically as the subjugation of rights to right as a set of rites—the rituals of rule (Foucault 1991). As Foucault (1980) explained of "truth," rights are "types of discourse which it accepts and makes function as true" (131). Rights are not exchanged, but exercised: Rights exist "in action" and thus in order to "defend human rights," we must first examine how they are practiced. Human rights work is not practiced *on rights*; human rights work is practiced *as right* on people who are monitored, measured, used, and valorized. This rarely has anything to do with "defending human rights"; it has everything to do with human management. In practice, all human rights are reduced to the performance of the right rites, which is currently the manufacture of knowledge that suppresses alternative versions of right, and thus it is the manufacture of power.

If, as Luke (1998) argues, "rule boils down to giving commands, and getting compliance with them—by consent or coercion—from those who are ruled…. The practices of ruling are the in-statement of rules concocted from the arts of covenant …" (10), then rule is exercised as effectively, if not more effectively, by contragovernmentalized NGOs in the name of human rights as it was by the nation-state. We can understand the practice of commands as emerging from a *knowledge that commands action*. Compliance with the human rights regime of *rule by rite* is thus *epistemological compliance*. This is so because epistemology is powerful, political, and contestable, whether exercised through governmentality or consolidated contragovernmentality, the nation-state or cosmopolitanism. If ruling is achieved through knowledge, then knowledge is where we must transform the relations of rule.

When human rights are conflated with development, knowledge is imposed through administration on those NGOs and other actors assigned with the certification of human rights as right, resulting in development dominating rights through the assertion of shared rites. As Marie Campbell and Ann Manicom (1995) argue: "Administration, management, and government are accomplished through work processes that rely on distinctively organized ways of knowing those aspects of the world that are to be ruled. Not only does ruling *rely on* specialized knowledge, but a central task of ruling is to *organize and generate knowledge in a form that is useful for ruling practice*" (9).

An empirical investigation of organization and generation of specialized knowledge in relationship to human rights is warranted. Here I offer a limited sample of statements on the right (correct) practice of human rights as they are produced by the global cosmopolitan governance regime, which, according to the Office of the United Nations High Commission for Human Rights (OHCHR) (2008a), includes NGOs, the UN, nation-states, corporations, and IGOs such as World Bank. This regime dictates what I understand as the rituals of rite as they are practiced as rites of rule. I aim to observe how the human rights regime proposes that we properly know human rights. Given Burawoy's (2006) emphasis on NGOs as the saviours/*savoirs* of human rights, I focus here on the role of NGOs within the human rights regime of rite. The OHCHR (2008b) Civil Society Unit specifically addresses NGOs as "relevant stakeholders" in human rights and provides NGOs with a handbook on the rituals of rite: "The Handbook aims to provide NGOs with a comprehensive and user-friendly guide to the work of OHCHR, including key information on human rights mechanisms, entry points for NGOs and contact details with a view to assisting NGOs in identifying areas of possible cooperation and partnership with OHCHR." This guide to the rites of OHCHR specifies the rituals associated with the rites of passage to human rights as instrumental rites, defined by OHCHR. The following observations emphasize a sample of the employment of instrumental rites within the OHCHR in order to demonstrate that, like governmentality, consolidated contragovernmentality achieves "security, territory, and population" by ensuring "the emergence of population as datum, as a field of intervention and as an objective of governmental techniques" (Foucault 1991, 102).

This first observation (Box 7-1) highlights the way in which human rights are monitored as expert (exclusionary) and instrumental (productive) rites, including: *monitoring, experts, instruments, legal status, standard rules, undeniable moral force, conduct, mandate,* and *compliance.* These are terms generally associated with discipline and control rather than with human well-being. These instruments are a rationality of rights and, like all administrative reforms, administer human rights as though the tools that it uses to do so can somehow stand apart from the tools that were used to deny human rights in the first place. Human rights are not necessarily denied as a result of disorganization, and their reorganization ignores that the denial of human well-being has often been done in the name of "efficiency" and "organization." The tools for efficient power are the tools of human rights-cum-development rites: "time tables, collective training exercises, total and detailed surveillance"

Box 7-1 Establishment of Human Rights Bodies as Instruments of Monitoring

---

The Core International Human Rights Instruments and Their Monitoring Bodies There are nine core international human rights treaties. Each of these treaties has established a committee of *experts* to *monitor* implementation of the treaty provisions by its States parties....

Universal Human Rights Instruments [T]here are many other universal *instruments* relating to human rights....The *legal status* of these instruments varies: declarations, principles, guidelines, standard rules and recommendations have no binding legal effect, but such instruments have an *undeniable moral force* and provide practical guidance to States in their *conduct*....

Human Rights Bodies The Office of the High Commissioner for Human Rights (OHCHR) works to offer the best expertise and support to the different human rights *monitoring mechanisms* in the United Nations system: UN Charter-based bodies, including the Human Rights Council, and bodies created under the international human rights treaties and made up of *independent experts mandated to monitor* State parties' *compliance* with their treaty obligations.... (OHCHR 2008b, my emphasis and formatting)

(Foucault 1995, 220). The rise of disciplinary society parallels the rise of the practices of development. "In a word, the disciplines are the ensemble of minute technical inventions that made it possible to increase the useful size of multiplicities by decreasing the inconveniences of the power which, in order to make them useful, must control them" (Foucault 1995, 220). As Foucault (1995) observed, the state apparatus co-opts schools, churches, and now human rights organizations, in its surveillance. The discipline of human rights "swarms" in its flexibility (211). The UN practice of human rights is virtually indistinguishable from disciplinary society. The rise of the science of training the individual to be useful, of applying the individual to some "great essential function" (211), is the very science of human rights-cum-development.

Foucault's (1980) discussion of power/knowledge directly addresses the demand by the United Nations that experts "produce the truth of power that our society demands, of which it has need, in order to function: we *must* speak the truth; we are constrained or condemned to confess or to discover the truth. Power never ceases its interrogation, its inquisition, its registration of truth: it institutionalises, professionalises and rewards its pursuit" (93). The human rights expert is the conveyor of power as right. The boundary between human rights, which are the practice of knowledge, and power exercised as discipline is thus blurred. This is, of course, a point recognized not only by Foucault, but by all critical theories of the state in that critical theories of the state identify the ideological state apparatus, which does not exclude human rights organizations and the institutions charged with generating knowledge of rights.

This second observation (Box 7-2) of the Universal Periodic Review describes the means by which the OHCHR enforces rights according to official knowledge and tools for management of the population: written reports conforming to a preestablished standard (and thus in the terms of the regime of rite in accordance with rule), relevance, procedures, observations, credibility, and reliability.

The creation of official knowledge and language to discuss and evaluate human rights declares a boundary around what ought to be known about human rights and how it ought to be known. These boundaries are then monitored by those who have already falsely assumed that they have legitimate authority to construct discursive territory as though constructing discursive territory is not one of the most fundamental human rights. "All spaces are reconstructed out of human discourse" (Luke 1998, 3). The OHCHR has thus already excluded most human beings from the right to choose the terms according to which their rights will be discussed.

This observation (Box 7-3) is of the establishment of proper knowledge, which usually is only possessed by the most elite of any given society. Through the use of proper and improper formatting, language, knowledge, content, and, especially, key words, the OHCHR excludes improper and perhaps transformative knowledge as it employs rites as a basis for exclusion and delegitimization of those whose rights are governed by the right rules of rite. Participation is specifically contingent on *arrangements and practices observed by the Commission on Human Rights*—an organization must have official letterhead, identity must be validated and secure, and submissions must be appropriately and technically formatted according to specified boundaries. These review mechanisms are based in already existing practices and full cooperation that prescripts content, ways of knowing, and language.

Rites of passage to development thus require compliance with official knowledge. If we return to Foucault's (1980) understanding of the relationship between power, right, and truth, "what rules of right are implemented by the relations of power in the production of discourses of truth? ... We are subjected to the production of truth, through power and we cannot exercise power except through the production of truth" (93), the OHCHR is exposed as producing the truth of human rights through power. Power is exercised as the required truth for the rite of passage to development *via* human rights, which in turn become indistinguishable from the supposed *right* to development. These rituals of right(s) impose development's instrumental rationality as a relation of domination (Horkheimer and Adorno 1989).

Box 7-2 Organization for Rites of Review

In accordance with Resolution 5/1, the documents on which the review would be based are:

Information prepared by the State concerned, which can take the form of a national report, and any other *information considered relevant* by the State concerned, which could be presented either orally or in writing. The written presentation summarizing the information *shall not exceed 20 pages,* and should be submitted six weeks prior to the session of the Working Group at which the specific review will take place. States are encouraged to prepare the information through a broad consultation process at the national level with all *relevant stakeholders.*

Additionally a compilation prepared by the OHCHR of the information contained in the reports of treaty bodies, special procedures, including *observations* and comments by the State concerned, and other relevant official United Nations documents, which shall not exceed 10 pages;

Additional, *credible and reliable information provided by other relevant stakeholders* to the universal periodic review which should also be taken into consideration by the Council in the review, which will be summarized by the OHCHR in a document that shall not exceed 10 pages. Stakeholders include, inter alia, NGOs, NHRIs, Human rights defenders, Academic institutions and Research institutes, Regional organizations, as well as civil society representatives. (OHCHR 2008c, my emphasis and formatting)

Box 7-3 Certifying Rite as Right, NGOs as Participants in the Rites of Passage

---

Accreditation of NGOs … the *participation of NGOs in the Human Rights Council shall be based on the arrangements and practices observed by the Commission on Human Rights,* including Economic and Social Council resolution 1996/31 of 25 July 1996. NGOs in consultative status with ECOSOC wishing to accredit representatives to the first session of the UPR working group are invited to send their letter of accreditation request/s to the Secretariat of the Council.…

The letter requesting accreditation should contain the following elements: It should be submitted on the *official letterhead* of the organization; It should clearly state the title and duration of the session the organization wishes to attend, e.g. 'Name of NGO, in consultative status with ECOSOC, wishes to send the following members to attend the 1st session of the UPR working group …'; The letter needs to be signed by the President or the Main Representative of the organization in Geneva; It should also indicate the name/s (first name and family name) of the person/s who will represent the organization at the HRC session: Names of persons must appear exactly as they appear in the *ID document,* Family Name(s) have to be capitalized.… It is important to ensure that the name(s) of those members already in possession of a *valid identity* badge issued by UNOG Security and Safety Section, and who plan to attend the first session of the UPR working group, is/are also included in the accreditation letter, with an indication that the person(s) hold(s) an annual badge. Annual or temporary representatives of NGOs in possession of an identity badge issued by UNOG Security and Safety Section and valid for the duration of the session, will have unrestricted access to the conference rooms.… (OHCHR 2008d)

The rite of passage to human rights as development requires receiving, through rituals of rite, what Horkheimer and Adorno (1989) recognized as the myth of enlightenment: modernity's religion. Human rights as the rite of passage to a stage of development enchanted by the UN is just such an Enlightenment practice, banishing "fear of the unknown by evaluating the world with respect to the operational norms of 'computation and utility' … rejects that which cannot be quantified and measured. In this way, science is less open-minded than its partisans contend; indeed, science is a new form of ancient mythology" (Horkheimer and Adorno 1989, 6). Through the rituals of counting, monitoring, and accreditation, the OHCHR, like enlightenment:

> treats its own ideas of human rights exactly as it does the older universals. Every spiritual resistance it encounters serves merely to increase its strength. Which means that enlightenment still recognizes itself even in its myths. Whatever myths the resistance may appeal to, by virtue of the very fact that they become argument in the process of opposition, they acknowledge the principle of

dissolvent rationality for which they reproach the Enlightenment. Enlightenment is totalitarian. (Horkheimer and Adorno 1989, 6)

Anti-enlightenment conceptions of humanity and its well-being are excluded based on their incalculability.

These rites of rule depend on an epistemological hierarchy that knows human rights according to their use value: OHCHR knows human rights not only through the same rites as the economy and security, but according to what must be known in order for the "developed" world to legitimately interact with the "undeveloped" world through the exchange of capital. The cosmopolitan global governance regime, acting on behalf of the global movement of capital through rituals of rite, *depends on* the guise of human rights in order to legitimate domination and exploitation as humanitarian action.

Public sociology for human rights as it has evolved thus far has been conflated with development and officialdom as they are embodied in the OHCHR's rites of rule, resulting in a public sociology that, in practice, would legitimate the shift from governmentality to consolidated contragovernmentality. We ought to question any discussion of public sociology for human rights that bypasses an analysis of disciplinary rites as it shifts the legitimating narrative of sovereignty to the equally legitimating narrative of human rights, dispersing governmentality more widely into increasingly infinitesimal contragovernmentalities of rule without ever shifting the *practice* of the *techniques* of rule, which are born of knowledge. These contragovernmental human rights as rites of rule function according to the mythical rite of passage from an immature underdeveloped state to development-as-maturity achieved through the rites of instrumental knowledge exercised through the OHCHR's monitoring bodies. Yet, development is a fundamentally immature stance on the necessity of control based in the belief that the exercise of instrumental knowledge necessarily liberates rather than dominates. The myth of knowledge liberating humanity through infinite control and monitoring is an expectation of the most underdeveloped sort. Uncritically receiving the rites of enlightenment as they are practiced by OHCHR only forestalls the realization that human rights can only be attained *outside* of instrumental rationality because instrumentalized humanity is disciplined and often exploited humanity.

Our task in regard to human rights is therefore to *distinguish* human rights from development and thus to *deny* the myth that the only path to well-being is to sell one's labor and land according to the rules set by global capital. It is possible to resist the terms *relevant, official, standardized, legitimate,* and *expert,* as they are employed and enforced within the regime of rite. However, this resistance requires exposure of the everyday realities specifically excluded from OHCHR's practice of human rights as rites of rule, which excludes the knowledge inherent to the irrelevant, the unofficial, the illegitimate, and quotidian expertise about the human condition. Public sociology for human rights is deeply implicated in such exclusions to the extent that it ossifies the knowledge boundaries by which they are achieved, but it also can be responsible for dissolving them. Knowledge and the relations of practice that it orders are contestable. There is therefore significant space within which sociologists can maneuver in order to contest the construction of human rights as the rites of rule. A "public sociology for human rights" must stand apart from the "rights of rule," cease provision of the legitimating logics for consolidated contragovernmentality, and instead focus on the ways in which the rituals of rite according to the mythology of development facilitate the denial of well-being.

Notes

1. Burawoy (2006) acknowledges that there is a "bad humanitarianism" (5), but fails to explain why or how it is that his own humanitarianism can be distinguished from it.

2. Here Burawoy has contradicted his earlier (2005a) call for a division of labor for sociology, which included the reification of policy sociologists.

Chapter 8

Conclusion

Beyond Knowledge Production as the Reproduction of the Present

Ralph Waldo Emerson famously remarked: "What you do speaks so loud that I cannot hear what you say." In the case of public sociology, civil society, and governance, the opposite might be true; what is said is so loud that we cannot see what is being done. Declarations of transformation govern as they divert our attention from, and thus preserve, the practice of power relations. This reveals the way in which *saying is doing*. This was recognized by Marx as praxis—the infusion of practice with ideational claims. The Frankfurt School and Foucault further recognized how praxis can also function as knowledge/power. If saying is doing and doing is powerful, why are some things said at a particular point in time? In other words, how do some stabilizing ontological claims (saying) achieve value in relationship to the practices of governing (doing), while others, which would be the basis for transformation, are dismissed?

The value of knowledge claims for the practice of governing brings us back to my initial inquiry into the "kinship between the lines of inquiry and the proximity of those who undertook them" (Foucault 1998: 439). In response to this inquiry, I have framed public sociology, civil society, and governance as three related statements on the contemporary practice of governing. These statements are allied through a regime of knowledge/power that imbues them with authority. If public sociology, civil society, and governance are more than ideals—if they not only "say," but also "do"—then the politics represented by these phrases cannot be located in their ideals alone; in order to understand how they relate to the regime of knowledge/ power that underpins contemporary governing, we have to understand the divergence of epistemological practice from ontological claims and how this practice relates to the inhibition of transformative imagination. Today, this means that we have to understand the divergence of the continuation of instrumental rationality from claims that democratic transformation is under way.

Public sociology, civil society, and *governance* make a confusing array of claims about how politics are organized in the contemporary moment. However, we can understand the interrelation of these terms by engaging them as a set of governing practices. These practices include: first, the reinforcing relationship between ontological claims and epistemological practice; second, the institutionalization of these claims and practices as legitimate knowledge production; and, third, the relationship of these claims and practices to the demands of contemporary governing. In each case considered here, an ontological claim was staked by an enterprising advocate: Burawoy claimed a sociological division of labor and the standpoint of civil society; Salamon claimed civil society as a discrete economic input known in terms of the number of organizational units; and Sørensen and Torfing claimed an era of radically democratic post-liberal governance known outside of the radicalization of practice. In each case these claims were then institutionalized and encoded in a particular epistemological orientation: The division of sociological labor institutionalized instrumental knowledge, which was subsequently encoded in public sociology curricula as performance and evaluation; the Center for Civil Society Studies Comparative Nonprofit Sector Project exercised instrumental knowledge over civil society, recreating human agency in the image of the market; the practice of network governance as instrumental rationality was stabilized behind a claim to radical democracy and was institutionalized as efficiency, effectiveness, and innovation by the Centre for Democratic Network Governance. Finally, in each case the practice of these institutionalized ontological claims contributed to the regime of knowledge/power that legitimates and stabilizes the contemporary practice of governing: Public sociology engages in artificial negativity as it frames resistance (public sociology) in the terms of that which it claims to resist (professional sociology); civil society takes over for civic culture as an "answer" to the problems of "democratic stability"; and network governance provides the "democratic anchorage" of neoliberal network governance.

Although they claim disciplinary distinction, the careers of public sociology, civil society, and governance are similarly structured. In Part I, I demonstrated how the unique progression of Burawoy's 2004 campaign for public sociology contributed to the legitimacy of his argument. This legitimacy is due in large part to Burawoy's association with the ASA and the widespread circulation of his work through publication networks that are highly valued for the purposes of career advancement in sociology. Although the critical ideal of public sociology was in circulation prior to his campaign, it was Burawoy who transformed it into a product that could be given value in relationship to present demands for the authority of knowledge and the stabilization of instrumental practices. Given the legitimacy that association with the ASA and publication contribute to knowledge, within five years of Burawoy's Presidential Address to the ASA, it was difficult to speak of public sociology without reference to Burawoy's model. By 2010, two ontological assumptions had been fortified: a division of sociological labor and a boundary between the state, market, and civil society.

This resulted in a third fortification: the *impression* that institutionalized sociology was embracing the politics of knowledge. Burawoy's campaign performed as artificial negativity; public sociology was advanced as a "counter-bureaucratic strategy," redirecting the impulse to criticize professional sociology back into a division of labor that served as its stabilization. As I argued in Chapter Three, the division of sociological labor was not only an argument for public sociology and reflexive knowledge, it was also an argument for professional sociology and instrumental knowledge. Although in his division of labor Burawoy claimed that instrumental knowledge would be limited to professional and policy sociology, it was instrumental knowledge that was institutionalized as an epistemological practice in the establishment of public sociology curricula. According to these curricula, public sociology in practice would involve decision making, research methods, program formulation and grant writing, evaluation, management of organizations and groups, and governance skills to be contributed to the state, the nonprofit sector, and think tanks. Public sociology in this institutionalization mirrors the production of the techniques of governing as they are institutionalized in the field of public administration and policy. In practice, therefore, the epistemological basis for practicing public sociology betrays both of Burawoy's ontological claims: that the division of labor preserves public sociology as reflexive rather than instrumental knowledge and that there is a boundary between civil society/sociology and the state/political science.

The evolution of the ideal of civil society follows a disciplinary path from critique to stabilization similar to that of public sociology. Although civil society circulated as a critical ideal in the late 1980s and early 1990s, it was Salamon's framing of civil society as NGO research and his widespread operationalization of the concept that facilitated its eventual success as a tool of governing practiced through funding regimes. The institutionalization of Salamon's campaign in the Johns Hopkins Center for Civil Society Studies, and its subsequent institutionalizations within national governments who were invited to participate in his projects, in many ways mirrors the institutionalization of public sociology within the ASA and public sociology curricula: Knowledge is given authority through "research skills" that can be "contributed" to the practice of governing. These research skills are then exercised over civil society as instrumental practice and control are pursued in the interest of "democratic stability." In the end, both public sociology and civil society are institutionalized as global NGO productivity, which is a powerful instrument of governing.

As with public sociology by Burawoy and civil society by Salamon, Sørensen and Torfing's campaign for "radically democratic network governance" circulated through a publishing blitz that advanced a definition, an analytical model, and an operationalization that lends itself easily to governing institutions. In their reference to post-liberalism, Sørensen and Torfing employ an ontological claim as the basis for the expansion of governing into non-state spaces and then proceed to stabilize the instrumental practices of governing—innovation, effectiveness, and efficiency—by saying so loudly that it is radical democracy that it is difficult to hear the practice of neoliberalism. The institutionalization of network governance as legitimate knowledge makes a contribution to the stabilization of governing in the form of the reproduction of instrumental knowledge, which is encoded with relations of power. It provides a legitimating narrative for the continuation of neoliberalism, while failing to challenge the epistemology according to which it is practiced. In its institutionalization, this knowledge claim achieves authority over possibility.

Although they claim a critical stance, public sociology, civil society, and governance have frequently conformed to contemporary demands for governing knowledge in a neoliberal era. In the case of public sociology, Burawoy has framed his campaign in opposition to neoliberalism, but has failed to frame public sociology in opposition to the authority of instrumental knowledge upon which neoliberalism depends. Further, his argument for a public sociology for human rights is simultaneously an argument for development rights; this position conforms precisely to Thatcher's emphasis on "freedoms" that facilitate the global expansion of capital. Thatcher's use of the ideal of civil society to explain neoliberal reforms as democratic transformations is further indicative of the relationship between civil society and neoliberalism. The subsequent operationalization and institutionalization of civil society as NGOs through the Johns Hopkins Center for Civil Society Studies provided a vehicle for the spread of these reforms, while simultaneously stripping the concept of its normative dimension. As the Comparative Nonprofit Sector Project recreated civil society in the image of the market, the neoliberal emphasis on "economic contribution" replaced democratic ideals. As public sociology and civil society in these institutionalizations stabilized instrumental knowledge production, "radically democratic network governance" provided a legitimating logic for neoliberalism's emphasis on making the state more flexible and responsive to the needs of the market through the deinstitutionalization of government and its dispersal through networks. This "flexibility" is anchored by Sørensen and Torfing in post-Marxism's logic of post-liberalism, which allows for them to assert the continued instrumental practices of the state as legitimate, while claiming that neoliberal network governance represents a transformation of the state toward "radical democracy."

At the outset of this book I proposed that the intersection of public sociology, civil society, and governance posed a problem for advocates of a democratic transformation of the contemporary practice of governing. I do not oppose public sociology, civil society, or radically democratic governance as ideals to which we should aspire. I do, however, oppose the ways in which they have been practiced in the image of neoliberalism and in fulfillment of governing requirements for legitimating narratives of present power formations and instrumental knowledge production. When I first encountered them, I advocated these concepts as critical ideals. However, as I located their practices in the contemporary regime of knowledge and governing it became clear to me that it is not enough to advocate the vocabulary of public sociology, civil society, or radically democratic governance. In the first five years of my academic career, I was an advocate of Agger's concept of public sociology. I later found that I could not advocate "public sociology" as it has been institutionalized, because in circulation it represented a division of academic labor that I knew not to exist and that was aimed at stabilizing ontological and epistemological assumptions with which I did not agree. When as a PhD student I first began working on grant-funded projects that were dedicated to "building democracy" in Eastern Europe, I was an advocate of the concept of civil society and envisioned grassroots organizations debating what "democracy" would mean. I, like Arato, observed this in some places outside of the academy, but as I worked with local governments and nonprofits in Central and Eastern Europe and in the Antipodes, at nearly every turn, I was faced with Lester Salamon "putting civil society on the economic map of the world." I quickly discovered that I could not advocate the ideal of civil society as it had been institutionalized, because it represented an instrumental attempt to make humanity conform to the market. I could participate in projects dedicated to "building civil society," but in most cases this involved either transferring neoliberal techniques for governing or purchasing translated datasheets containing the names of nonprofits registered with the state. I did both of these things, and neither of them had any impact on what I envisioned to be civil society; it seemed to me that the impact that I made was to keep smart people busy reproducing an image of democracy that originated in a philanthropic foundation or academic institute several time zones and exchange rates away from the reality of their everyday lives. Because I was initially trained in the field of public administration, I was a bit wiser when I first encountered the phrase "radical democratic governance," and I immediately recognized it as fundamentally continuous with the practice of "government." I have yet to encounter an institutionalized governance network that I could describe as radically democratic.

My tentative conclusion based on these varying encounters with varying explanations of governing is that there are no words, ideas, or modes of organization that will guarantee democracy. Easy solutions are available in the narratives of public sociology, civil society, and governance, but these solutions fail to solve the problem of the disciplinary impact of the authority of governing knowledge on our everyday lives. As I demonstrated in Part III, the problem is not that there is knowledge involved in governing, but that the instrumental knowledge that is currently practiced functions powerfully as discipline and domination. It certainly is possible to engage in a critical intellectuality toward these ideals, one that challenges those portrayals that preserve unnecessarily oppressive relations of power that deny people the opportunity to change the circumstances that impact their everyday lives. The dead ends that I encountered when pursuing a path of transformative intellectuality through the practice of public sociology, civil society, and governance do not indicate that there is no place to go. Knowledge about how to transform society is produced by critical intellectuals who do not get grants, uncounted practitioners who make unfunded countergovernmental impacts through NGOs, and non-state organizations that do not "count" because they do not possess the knowledge,, skills,, and "legitimacy" required to participate in governance networks. The challenge is to value this knowledge as the legitimate contribution that it is.

At the very least, we can say that, in their practiced intersections, public sociology, civil society, and governance reveal that disciplinary distinctions no longer warrant the authority that they claim. There is virtually no distinction to be made among the governing techniques that are legitimated by these various labels. The contestability of the power relations embedded in the techniques of governing ought to speak more loudly than their legitimation. In making this argument, I am recommending that the intellectual approach to these concepts ought to be grounded in critical theory, which seeks not to reproduce, but to transform contemporary relations of power as they are preserved and practiced through knowledge production.

References

Abrams, Philip. "Notes on the Difficulty of Studying the State." *Journal of Historical Sociology* 1 (1988): 58–89.

Agger, Anikka, Eva Sørensen, and Jacob Torfing. "It Takes Two to Tango: When Public and Private Actors Interact." In *Civic Engagement in a Network Society*, edited by Kaifeng Yang and Erik Bergrud, 15–40. Charlotte, NC: Information Age Publishing, 2008.

Agger, Ben. *Fast Capitalism: A Critical Theory of Significance*. Urbana: University of Illinois Press, 1989a.

———. *Socio(onto)logy: A Disciplinary Reading*. Urbana: University of Illinois Press, 1989b.

———. *Reading Science: A Literary, Political, and Sociological Analysis*. Dix Hills, NY: General Hall, Inc, 1989c.

———. "Is Wright Wrong (or Should Burawoy be Buried)?: Reflections on the Crisis of the 'Crisis of Marxism'." *Berkeley Journal of Sociology* 33 (1989d): 187–207.

———. *The Decline of Discourse: Reading, Writing and Resistance in Postmodern Capitalism*. New York: The Falmer Press, 1990.

———. "Critical Theory, Poststructuralism, Postmodernism: Their Sociological Relevance." *Annual Review of Sociology* 17 (1991a): 105–131.

———. *A Critical Theory of Public Life: Knowledge, Discourse, and Politics in an Age of Decline*. London: Routledge Falmer, 1991b.

———. *The Discourse of Domination: From the Frankfurt School to Postmodernism*. Evanston, IL: Northwestern University Press, 1992a.

———. *Cultural Studies as Critical Theory*. London: Falmer Press, 1992b.

———. *Gender, Culture, Power: Toward a Feminist Postmodern Critical Theory*. Westport, CT: Praeger, 1993.

———. *Public Sociology: From Social Facts to Literary Acts*. New York: Rowman and Littlefield Publishers, 2000.

———. *Public Sociology: From Social Facts to Literary Acts*, 2nd ed. New York: Rowman and Littlefield Publishers, 2007.

Agger, Ben, and Timothy W. Luke. "Politics in Postmodernity: The Diaspora of Politics and the Homelessness of Political and Social Theory." *Theoretical Discussions in Political Sociology for the 21st Century* 11 (2002): 159–195.

Ahmed, Shamima, and David M. Potter. *NGOs in International Politics.* West Hartford, CT: Kumarian Press Inc., 2006.

Aksartova, Sada. "Why NGOs? How American Donors Embraced Civil Society After the Cold War." *International Journal of Not-for-Profit Law* 8 (2006): 16–21.

Alexander, Jeffrey C. "The Paradoxes of Civil Society." *International Sociology* 12 (1997): 115–133.

Almond, Gabriel A. "The Return to the State." *The American Political Science Review* 82 (Sept. 1988): 853–874.

Almond, Gabriel A.. and Sidney Verba. *The Civic Culture: Political Attitudes and Democracy in Five Countries.* Princeton, NJ: Princeton University Press, 1963.

Alston, Philip, and Mary Robinson. *Human Rights and Development: Towards Mutual Reinforcement.* Oxford: Oxford University Press, 2005.

American University. *MA Concentration in Public Sociology.* http://www.american.edu/cas/sociology/maps/. (Accessed November 22, 2007.)

American University. *Graduate Certificate in Public Sociology.* http://www.american.edu/cas/sociology/CERT-GPSOC.cfm. (Accessed November 22, 2010.)

Ansell, Chris, and Alison Gash. "Collaborative Governance in Theory and Practice." *Journal of Public Administration Research and Theory* 18 (2008): 543–571.

Apple, Michael W. *Official Knowledge: Democratic Education in a Conservative Age.* New York: Routledge, 1993.

———, ed. *The State and the Politics of Knowledge.* New York: RoutledgeFalmer, 2003.

Arato, Andrew. "Civil Society Against the State: Poland 1980–1981." *Telos* 47 (Spring, 1981): 23–47.

Arato, Andrew, and Jean Cohen. "Civil Society and Social Theory." *Thesis Eleven* 21 (1988): 40–64.

Aronowitz, Stanley. *The Knowledge Factory: Dismantling the Corporate University and Creating True Higher Learning.* Boston, MA: Beacon Press, 2000.

———. "A Mills Revival?" *Logos* 2.3 (2003).

Aronowitz, Stanley, and Peter Bratsis, eds. *Paradigm Lost: State Theory Reconsidered.* Minneapolis: University of Minnesota Press, 2002.

ASA Task Force on Institutionalizing Public Sociologies. "Public Sociology and the Roots of American Sociology: Re-Establishing our Connections to the Public. Interim Report and Recommendations." Submitted to the ASA Council July 2005. http://pubsoc.wisc.edu/05report.html. (Accessed December 1, 2010.)

———. "Standards of Public Sociology: Guidelines for Use by Academic Departments in Personnel Reviews." February 2007. http://www.imaginingamerica.org/IApdfs/pubsocstandards20070809.pdf. (Accessed December 1, 2010.)

Auden, W. H. "Archaeology." *Selected Poems,* expanded edition, edited by Edward Mendelson. New York: Vintage International, 2007.

Baccaro, Lucio. "Civil Society Meets the State: Towards Associational Democracy?" *Socio-Economic Review* 4 (2006): 185–208.

Ball, Colin, and Barry Knight. "Why We Must Listen to Citizens." In *Civil Society at the Millennium,* edited by Kumi Naidoo, 17–26. West Hartford, CT: Kumarian Press. Inc., 1999.

Barrow, Clyde W. "Intellectuals in Contemporary Social Theory: A Radical Critique." *Sociological Inquiry* 57 (Fall, 1987): 415–430.

————. *Universities and the Capitalist State: Corporate Liberalism and the Reconstruction of American Higher Education, 1894–1928.* Madison: University of Wisconsin Press, 1990.

————. *Critical Theories of the State: Marxist, Neo-Marxist, Post-Marxist.* Madison: The University of Wisconsin Press, 1993.

Beck, Ulrich. *Power in the Global Age.* Cambridge: Polity, 2005a.

————. "How Not to Become a Museum Piece." *British Journal of Sociology* 56 (2005b): 335–343.

Benhabib, Seyla. *Critique, Norm, and Utopia: A Study of the Foundations of Critical Theory.* New York: Columbia University Press, 1986.

Best, Steven, and Douglas Kellner. *Postmodern Theory: Critical Interrogations.* New York: The Guilford Press, 1991.

Blank, Robert H. *Brain Policy: How the New Neuroscience Will Change Our Lives and Our Politics.* Washington, DC: Georgetown University Press, 1999.

Blau, Judith, and Keri E. I. Smith, eds. *The Public Sociologies Reader.* Lanham, MD: Rowman and Littlefield Publishers, 2006.

Blomgren Bingham, Lisa, Tina Nabatchi, and Rosemary O'Leary. "The New Governance: Practices and Processes for Stakeholder and Citizen Participation in the Work of Government." *Public Administration Review* 65 (2005): 547–558.

Boli, John, and George M. Thomas. *Constructing World Culture: International Non-governmental Organizations Since 1875.* Stanford, CA: Stanford University Press, 1999.

Boltanski, Luc, and Eve Chiapello. *The New Spirit of Capitalism.* New York: Verso, 2005.

Borofsky, Robert. "Public Anthropology: Where to? What Next?" *Anthropology News* (2000): 9–10.

Box, Richard. C. *Critical Social Theories in Public Administration.* Armonk, NY: M. E. Sharpe, 2005.

Box, Richard C., and Cheryl S. King. "The 'T'ruth is Elsewhere: Critical History." *Administrative Theory and Praxis* 22 (2000): 751–771.

Boyns, David, and Jesse Fletcher. "Reflections on Public Sociology: Public Relations, Disciplinary Identity, and the Strong Program in Professional Sociology." In *Public Sociology: The Contemporary Debate,* edited by Lawrence T. Nichols, 119–148. New Brunswick, NJ: Transaction Publishers, 2007.

Bratsis, Peter. "Unthinking the State: Reification, Ideology and the State as a Social Fact." In *Paradigm Lost: State Theory Reconsidered,* edited by Stanley Aronowitz and Peter Bratsis, 247–267. Minneapolis: University of Minnesota Press, 2002.

————. *Everyday Life and the State.* Boulder, CO: Paradigm Publishers, 2006.

Brint, Steven. "Guide for the Perplexed." In *Public Sociology: The Contemporary Debate,* edited by Lawrence T. Nichols, 237–262. New Brunswick, NJ: Transaction Publishers, 2007.

Bryant, Christopher G. A. "Social Self-Organization, Civility and Sociology: A Comment on Kumar's 'Civil Society'." *British Journal of Sociology* 44 (1993): 397–401.

Burawoy, Michael. "Marxism, Philosophy and Science." *Berkeley Journal of Sociology* 33 (1989): 223–249.

————. "Introduction, Public Sociologies: A Symposium from Boston College." *Social Problems* 51 (2004a): 103–106.

———. "Manifesto for Public Sociologies." *Social Problems* 51 (2004b): 124–130.

———. "Public Sociologies: Contradictions, Dilemmas, and Possibilities." *Social Forces* 82 (2004c): 1603–1618.

———. "The World Needs Public Sociology." *Sosiologisk Tidsskrift* 12 (2004d): 255–272.

———. "2004 American Sociological Association Presidential Address: For Public Sociology." *American Sociological Review* 70 (2005a): 4–28.

———. "Public Sociology: Populist Fad or Path to Renewal?" *British Journal of Sociology* 56 (2005b): 417–432.

———. "The Critical Turn to Public Sociology." *Critical Sociology* 31 (2005c): 313–326.

———. "Introduction: A Public Sociology for Human Rights." In *Public Sociologies Reader,* edited by Judith Blau and Keri E. I. Smith, 1–18. Lanham, MD: Rowman and Littlefield Publishers, 2006.

———. "For Public Sociology." In *Public Sociology: Fifteen Eminent Sociologists Debate Politics and the Profession in the Twenty-first Century,* edited by Dan Clawson, Robert Zussman, Joya Misra, Naomi Gerstel, Randall Stokes, Douglas L. Anderton, and Michael Burawoy, 23–64. Berkeley: University of California Press, 2007a.

———. "The Field of Sociology: Its Power and Its Promise." In *Public Sociology: Fifteen Eminent Sociologists Debate Politics and the Profession in the Twenty-first Century,* edited by Dan Clawson, Robert Zussman, Joya Misra, Naomi Gerstel, Randall Stokes, Douglas L. Anderton, and Michael Burawoy, 241–258. Berkeley: University of California Press, 2007b.

———. "Public Sociology vs. The Market." *Socio-Economic Review* 52 (2007c): 356–367.

———. "Third-Wave Sociology and the End of Pure Science." In *Public Sociology: The Contemporary Debate,* edited by Lawrence T. Nichols, 317–335. New Brunswick, NJ: Transaction Publishers, 2007d.

———. "Public Sociology: Mills vs. Gramsci: Introduction to the Italian Translation of 'For Public Sociology'." *Sociologica* 1 (2007e): 7–13.

———. "What Is To Be Done? Theses on the Degradation of Social Existence in a Globalizing World." *Current Sociology* 56 (2008): 351–359.

———. "The Public Sociology Wars." In *Handbook of Public Sociology,* edited by Vincent Jeffries, 449–473. Lanham, MD: Rowman & Littlefield Publishers, 2009a.

———. "Public Sociology in the Age of Obama." *Innovation: The European Journal of Social Science Research* 22 (2009b): 189–199.

Calhoun, Craig, ed. *Habermas and the Public Sphere.* Cambridge: MIT Press, 1992.

———. "Civil Society and the Public Sphere." *Public Culture* 5 (1993): 267–280.

———. *Critical Social Theory.* Oxford: Blackwell, 1995.

———. "The Promise of Public Sociology." *British Journal of Sociology* 56 (2005): 355–363.

———. "The University and the Public Good." *Thesis Eleven* 84, no. 1 (2006): 7–43.

———. "Social Science for Public Knowledge." In *Academics as Public Intellectuals,* edited by Sven Eliaeson and Ragnvald Kalleberg, 299–318. London: Palgrave, 2008.

Campbell, Marie, and Ann Manicom. "Introduction." In *Knowledge, Experience, and Ruling Relations; Studies in the Social Organization of Knowledge,* edited by Marie Campbell and Ann Manicom, 3–17. Toronto: Toronto University Press, 1995.

Carr, Sarah. "Participation, Power, Conflict, and Change: Theorizing Dynamics of

Service User Participation in the Social Care System of England and Wales." *Critical Social Policy* 2 (2007): 266–276.

Castells, Manuel. "The New Public Sphere: Global Civil Society, Communication Networks, and Global Governance." *The ANNALS of the American Academy of Political and Social Science* 616 (2008): 78–93.

Catlaw, Thomas J. "Constitution as Executive Order: The Administrative State and the Political Ontology of 'We the People'." *Administration and Society* 37 (2005): 445–482.

———. "Performance Anxieties: Shifting Public Administration from the Relevant to the Real." *Administrative Theory & Praxis* 28 (2006): 89–120.

———. *Fabricating the People: Politics and Administration in the Biopolitical State.* Tuscaloosa: The University of Alabama Press, 2007.

Center for Civil Society Studies (CCSS). *The Johns Hopkins Center for Civil Society Studies.* http://www.ccss.jhu.edu/, 2010a.

———. *The New Governance Project.* http://www.ccss.jhu.edu, 2010b.

———. *Nonprofit Economic Data Project.* http://www.ccss.jhu.edu, 2010c.

———. *The Johns Hopkins University/International Labour Organization Volunteer Measurement Project.* http://www.ccss.jhu.edu, 2010d.

Centre for Democratic Network Governance. http://www.ruc.dk/forskning/forskningscentre/demnetgov/. (Accessed December 1, 2010.)

Chancer, Lynn, and Eugene McLaughlin. "Public Criminologies: Diverse Perspectives on Academia and Policy." *Theoretical Criminology* 11 (2007): 155–173.

Chandhoke, Neera. "The 'Civil' and the 'Political' in Civil Society." *Democratization* 8 (2001): 1–24.

———. "The Limits of Global Civil Society." In *Global Civil Society*, edited by Marlies Glasius, Mary Kaldor, and Helmut Anheier, 35–53. Oxford: Oxford University Press, 2002.

———. *The Conceits of Civil Society.* New Delhi: Oxford University Press, 2003.

Chatterjee, Partha. "A Response to Taylor's 'Modes of Civil Society'." *Public Culture* 3 (1990): 119–132.

Clawson, Dan, Robert Zussman, Joya Misra, Naomi Gerstel, Randall Stokes, Douglas L. Anderton, and Michael Burawoy, eds. *Public Sociology: Fifteen Eminent Sociologists Debate Politics and the Profession in the Twenty-first Century.* Berkeley: University of California Press, 2007.

Clegg, Stewart. "Foundations of Organization Power." *Journal of Power* 2, no. 1 (2009): 35–64.

Cohen, Joshua, and Joel Rogers. *Associations and Democracy.* London: Verso, 1995.

Cohen, Patricia. "In Tough Times, the Humanities Must Justify Their Worth." *The New York Times*, February 25 (2009), C1.

Comte, Auguste. "System of Positive Polity." In *On Intellectuals: Theoretical Studies Case Studies*, edited by Phillip Rieff, 248–282. Garden City, NY: Doubleday & Company, Inc., 1969.

———. *Introduction to Positive Philosophy*, edited and translated by Frederick Ferre. Indianapolis: Hackett Publishing Company 1988.

Corry, Olaf. "Defining and Theorizing the Third Sector." In *Third Sector Research*, edited by Rupert Taylor, 11–20. New York: Springer, 2010.

Cunliffe, Ann L., and Jong S. Jun. "The Need for Reflexivity in Public Administration." *Administration & Society* 37 (May 2005): 225–242.

Currie, Elliott. "Against Marginality: Arguments for a Public Criminology." *Theoretical Criminology* 11 (2007): 175–190.

Dahms, Harry. "How Social Science Is Impossible Without Critical Theory: The Immersion of Mainstream Approaches in Time and Space." In *No Social Science Without Critical Theory (Current Perspectives in Social Theory, Vol. 25)*, edited by Harry Dahms, 3–61. Emerald Group Publishing Limited, 2008.

Deflem, Mathieu. *Save Sociology!* http://www.savesociology.org/. (Accessed January 3, 2010.)

Delanty, Gerard. "Cosmopolitan Citizenship." In *Public Sociologies Reader,* edited by Judith Blau and Keri E. I. Smith, 37–50. Lanham, MD: Rowman and Littlefield Publishers, 2006.

Denhardt, Janet V., and Robert B. Denhardt. *The New Public Service: Serving, Not Steering.* New York: M. E. Sharpe, 2003.

Denhardt, Robert B. *In the Shadow of Organization.* Lawrence: The University of Kansas Press, 1981.

Department of Health. *Independence, Well-Being and Choice.* London: The Stationary Office, 2005.

Derber, Charles. "Public Sociology as a Vocation." *Social Problems* 51 (2004): 119–121.

Donahue, John. "On Collaborative Governance." Corporate Social Responsibility Initiative Working Paper No. 2. Cambridge, MA: John F. Kennedy School of Government, Harvard University, 2004.

Durkheim, Emile. *The Division of Labor in Society.* New York: Macmillan Company, 1933.

Ebrahim, Alnoor. "Accountability in Practice: Mechanisms for NGOs." *World Development* 31 (2003): 813–829.

———. "Placing the Normative Logics of Accountability in 'Thick' Perspective." *American Behavioral Scientist* 52 (2009): 885–904.

Ebrahim, Alnoor, and Edward Weisband, eds. *Global Accountabilities: Participation, Pluralism, and Public Ethics.* Cambridge: Cambridge University Press, 2007.

Edwards, Michael, and David Hulme, eds. *Beyond the Magic Bullet: NGO Performance and Accountability in the Post–Cold War World.* West Hartford, CT: Kumarian Press, 1996.

Edwards, Michael, and David Hulme. "NGO Performance and Accountability in the Post–Cold War World." *Journal of International Development* 7 (1995): 849–856.

———. "Too Close for Comfort? The Impact of Official Aid on Nongovermental Organizations." *World Development* 24 (1996): 961–973.

Ehrenberg, John. *Civil Society: The Critical History of an Idea.* New York: New York University Press, 1999.

el-Ojeili, Chamsy. "Post-Marxism with Substance: Castoriadis and the Autonomy Project." *New Political Science* 23 (2001): 225–239.

Ericson, Richard. "Publicizing Sociology." *British Journal of Sociology* 56 (2005): 365–372.

Esping-Andersen, Gøsta. *Three Worlds of Welfare Capitalism.* Princeton, NJ: Princeton University Press, 1990.

Etzioni, Amitai. "The Third Sector and Domestic Missions." *Public Administration Review* 33 (1973): 314–323.

Eulau, Heinz, Lucian Pye, and Sydney Verba. "In Memoriam: Gabriel A. Almond." *PS: Political Science and Politics* 36 (2003): 467–470.

Feagin, Joe. "Social Justice for Sociology: Agendas for the Twenty-First Century." *American Sociological Review* 66 (2001): 1–20.

Feagin, Joe, Sean Elias, and Jennifer Mueller. "Social Justice and Critical Public Sociology." In *Handbook of Public Sociology*, edited by Vincent Jeffries, 71–88. Lanham, MD: Rowman and Littlefield Publishers, 2009.

Foley, Michael W., and Bob Edwards. "The Paradox of Civil Society." *Journal of Democracy* 7 (1996): 38–52.

Ford Foundation. http://www.fordfoundation.org/. (Accessed December 3, 2010.)

———. *Report of the Study for the Ford Foundation on Policy and Program* (1949). http://www.fordfoundation.org/. (Accessed December 3, 2010.)

Foucault, Michel. *The Archaeology of Knowledge and the Discourse on Language.* Trans. A. M. Sheridan Smith. New York: Pantheon Books, 1972.

———. *The Birth of the Clinic: An Archaeology of Medical Perception.* New York: Pantheon, 1973.

———. "On Governmentality." *Ideology and Consciousness* 6 (Autumn, 1979): 5–21.

———. *Power/Knowledge: Selected Interviews and Other Writings 1972–1977,* edited and translated by Collin Gordon, translated by Leo Marshal, John Mepham, and Kate Sopher. New York: Pantheon Books, 1980.

———. "Governmentality." In *The Foucault Effect; Studies in Governmentality; With Two Lectures by and an Interview with Michel Foucault,* edited by Graham Burchell, Collin Gordon, and Peter Miller, 87–104. Chicago: The University of Chicago Press, 1991.

———. *Discipline and Punish: The Birth of the Prison,* translated by Alan Sheridan. New York: Vintage Books, 1995.

———. "Polemics, Politics, and Problematizations: An Interview with Michel Foucault." In *Ethics, Subjectivity and Truth. Essential works of Foucault 1954–1984 Vol. I,* edited by Paul Rabinow, 111–119. New York: The New Press, 1997.

———. "Structuralism and Post-Structuralism." In *Aesthetics, Method, and Epistemology,* edited by James D. Faubion, 433–458. New York: The New Press, 1998.

———. *The Order of Things: An Archaeology of the Human Sciences.* New York: Routledge, 2002.

Frankfurt Institute for Social Research. *Aspects of Sociology,* translated by John Vietrel. Boston, MA: Beacon Press, 1972.

Fraser, Nancy. *Unruly Practices: Power, Discourse, and Gender in Contemporary Social Theory.* Minneapolis: University of Minnesota Press, 1989.

———. "Rethinking the Public Sphere: A Contribution to the Critique of Actually Existing Democracy." In *Habermas and the Public Sphere,* edited by Craig Calhoun, 109–142. Cambridge: MIT Press, 1992.

———. "Transnational Public Sphere: Transnationalizing the Public Sphere: On the Legitimacy and Efficacy of Public Opinion in a Post-Westphalian World." *Theory, Culture, Society* 24 (2007): 7–30.

Fraser, Nancy, and Linda Gordon. "Contract Versus Charity: Why Is There No Social Citizenship in the United States?" *Socialist Review* 22, no. 3 (1992): 45–67.

Frederickson, George H. *New Public Administration.* Tuscaloosa: University of Alabama Press, 1980.

Fung, Archon. "Survey Article: Recipes for Public Spheres: Eight Institutional Design Choices and Their Consequences." *Journal of Political Philosophy* 11, no. 3 (2003): 338–367.

Gallagher, Charles A. "The Challenge to Public Sociology: Neoliberalism's Illusion of Inclusion." In *Public Sociologies Reader*, edited by Judith Blau and Keri E. I. Smith, 293–304. Lanham, MD: Rowman and Littlefield Publishers, 2006.

Gans, Herbert J. "Sociology in America: The Discipline and the Public." *American Sociological Review* 54 (1989): 1–16.

———. "A Sociology for Public Sociology: Some Needed Disciplinary Changes for Creating Public Sociology." In *Handbook of Public Sociology*, edited by Vincent Jeffries, 123–134. Lanham, MD: Rowman and Littlefield Publishers, 2009.

Gantman, Ernesto R. *Capitalism, Social Privilege and Managerial Ideologies*. Aldershot, UK: Ashgate Publishing, 2005.

Garcia-Zamor, Jean-Claude, and Renu Khator, eds. *Public Administration in the Global Village*. Westport, CT: Praeger, 1994.

Giddens, Anthony. *The Third Way: The Renewal of Social Democracy*. Cambridge: Polity, 2002.

Glenn, Evelyn N. "Whose Public Sociology? The Subaltern Speaks, but Who Is Listening?" In *Public Sociology: Fifteen Eminent Sociologists Debate Politics and the Profession in the Twenty-First Century*, edited by Dan Clawson, Robert Zussman, Joya Misra, Naomi Gerstel, Randall Stokes, Douglas L. Anderton, and Michael Burawoy, 213–229. Berkeley: University of California Press, 2007.

Goldsmith, Stephen, and William D. Eggers. *Governing by Network: The New Shape of the Public Sector*. Washington, DC: The Brookings Institution, 2004.

Goodnow, Frank J. *Politics and Administration: A Study in Government*. New York: Russell and Russell, 1900.

Gould, Kenneth A. "Promoting Sustainability." In *Public Sociologies Reader*, edited by Judith Blau and Keri E. I. Smith, 213–230. Lanham, MD: Rowman and Littlefield Publishers, 2006.

Gouldner, Alvin W. *The Coming Crisis of Western Sociology*. New York: Basic Books, 1970.

———. "Prologue to a Theory of Revolutionary Intellectuals." *Telos* 26 (1975–1976): 3–36.

Gramsci, Antonio. *Selections from the Prison Notebooks*, translated by Quintin Hoare and Geoffrey N. Smith. New York: International Publishers, 1997.

Gray, Mel, and Stephen A. Webb. "The Return of the Political in Social Work." *International Journal of Social Welfare* 18 (2009): 111–115.

Grey, Sandra, and Patricia M. Nickel. "Kiwibrand Resistance: Banking on Artificial Negativity." *Reconstruction: Studies in Contemporary Culture* 9, no. 4 (2009).

Gutmann, Amy, and Dennis F. Thompson. *Why Deliberative Democracy?* Princeton, NJ: Princeton University Press, 2004.

Habermas, Jurgen. *Toward a Rational Society*. London: Heinemann Educational Books Ltd, 1971.

———. *The Structural Transformation of the Public Sphere: An Inquiry into a Category of Bourgeois Society*, translated by Thomas Burger. Cambridge: The MIT Press, 1991.

Hall, John A. "A Guarded Welcome." *British Journal of Sociology* 56, no. 3 (2005): 379–381.

Haney, David Paul. *The Americanization of Social Science: Intellectuals and Public Responsibility in the Postwar United States.* Philadelphia, PA: Temple University Press, 2008.

Hardt, Michael, and Antonio Negri. *Empire.* Cambridge: Harvard University Press, 2000.

Harmon, Michael M. *Responsibility as Paradox: A Critique of Rational Discourse on Government.* Thousand Oaks, CA: SAGE Publications, Inc., 1995.

Harney, Stefano. *State Work: Public Administration and Mass Intellectuality.* Durham, MD: Duke University Press, 2002.

Harvard Committee. *General Education in a Free Society: Report of the Harvard Committee.* Cambridge, MA: Harvard University Press, 1945.

Harvey, David. *A Brief History of Neoliberalism.* Oxford: Oxford University Press, 2005, reprinted in paperback 2007.

———. *Spaces of Global Capitalism: Towards a Theory of Uneven Geographical Development.* New York: Verso, 2006.

Hauck, Robert J. P. "Editor's Note: On Public Intellectuals." *PS: Political Science and Politics,* October (2010): 649.

Hayden, Robert. "Dictatorships of Virtue? States, NGOs, and the Imposition of Democratic Values." *Harvard International Review* 24 (2002): 56–61.

Hilhorst, Dorothea. *The Real World of NGOs: Discourses, Diversity and Development.* London: Zed Books, 2003.

Hill, Carolyn J., and Laurence E. Lynn. "Is Hierarchical Governance in Decline? Evidence from Empirical Research." *Journal of Public Administration Research and Theory* 15 (2005): 173–195.

Hoggett, Paul. "Conflict, Ambivalence, and the Contested Purpose of Public Organizations." *Human Relations* 56 (2006): 175–194.

Horkheimer, Max. *Critical Theory: Selected Essays.* New York: Herder and Herder, 1972.

———. *Eclipse of Reason.* New York: Seabury, 1974.

Horkheimer, Max, and Theodor W. Adorno. *The Dialectic of Enlightenment.* Translation by John Cumming. New York: Herder and Herder, 1972.

———. *The Dialectic of Enlightenment.* Translation by John Cumming. New York: Continuum, 1989.

Howe, Barbara, and Emory Kemp. *Public History: An Introduction.* Malabar, FL: R. E. Krieger Publishing Company, 1986.

Humboldt State University. *Public Sociology, Ecological Justice and Action.* http://www.humboldt.edu/sociology/degrees/graduate.html. (Accessed November 22, 2010.)

Imber, Jonathan B. "Public Sociology: From Social Facts to Literary Acts." Review of *Public Sociology: From Social Facts to Literary Acts* by Ben Agger. *Social Forces* 80, no. 1 (2001): 353–354.

INCITE! Women of Color Against Violence. *The Revolution Will Not Be Funded: Beyond the Non-Profit Industrial Complex.* Cambridge, MA: South End Press, 2007.

Ivie, Robert L. "Rhetorical Deliberation and Democratic Politics in the Here and Now." *Rhetoric and Public Affairs* 5(2) (2002): 277–285.

Jacoby, Russell. *The Last Intellectuals: American Culture in the Age of Academe.* New York: Basic Books, 1987, reprinted in New York: Basic Books, 2000.

Jameson, Fredric. "Postmodernism, or the Cultural Logic of Late Capitalism." *New Left Review* 146 (1984): 53–92.

———. *The Cultural Turn: Selected Writings on the Postmodern: 1983–1998.* New York: Verso, 1998.

Jeffries, Vincent. "Pitirim A. Sorokin's Integralism and Public Sociology." In *Public Sociology: The Contemporary Debate,* edited by Lawrence T. Nichols, 149–178. New Brunswick, NJ: Transaction Publishers, 2007.

Jeffries, Vincent, ed. *Handbook of Public Sociology.* Lanham, MD: Rowman & Littlefield Publishers, 2009.

Jordan, Lisa, and Peter Van Tuijl, eds. *NGO Accountability: Politics, Principles & Innovations.* London: Earthscan, 2006.

Kaldor, Mary. *Global Civil Society: An Answer to War.* Cambridge: Polity Press, 2003.

Kaldor, Mary, Helmut Anheier, and Marlies Glasius, eds. *Global Civil Society 2004/2005.* London: Sage, 2005.

Kamat, Sangeeta. "NGOs and the New Democracy: The False Saviors of International Development." *Development and Modernization* 25 (2003): 65–69.

Keith, Michael. "Public Sociology: Between Heroic Immersion and Critical Distance: Personal Reflections on Academic Engagement with Political Life." *Critical Social Policy* 28 (2008): 320–334.

Kellner, Douglas. *Critical Theory, Marxism, and Modernity.* Baltimore: The Johns Hopkins University Press, 1989.

Kettl, Donald F. *The Transformation of Governance: Public Administration for Twenty-first Century America.* Baltimore, MD: The Johns Hopkins University Press, 2002.

King, Cheryl S., and Lisa A. Zanetti. *Transformational Public Service: Portraits of Theory in Practice.* New York: M. E. Sharpe, 2005.

Kovryga, O. V., and Patricia Nickel. "The Paradox of Decentralization Efforts in Ukraine." *Administrative Theory and Praxis* 26 (2004): 609–634.

———. "In a Cycle of False Necessity? Escaping from Embedded Quasi-Institutions and Building a New System of Public Administration and Management in Ukraine." *International Journal of Public Administration* 29 (2006): 1151–1166.

Kumar, Krishan. "Civil Society: An Inquiry into The Usefulness of An Historical Term." *British Journal of Sociology* 44 (1993): 375–395.

Laclau, Ernesto, and Chantal Mouffe. *Hegemony and Socialist Strategy: Towards a Radical Democratic Politics.* London: Verso, 2001.

Levine, Rhonda F., ed. *Enriching the Sociological Imagination: How Radical Sociology Changed the Discipline.* Leiden: Brill Academic Press, 2004.

Loveman, Brian. "The Comparative Administration Group, Development Administration, and Antidevelopment." *Public Administration Review* 36 (1976): 616–621.

Lowenstein, Karl. "Report on the Research Panel on Comparative Government." *American Political Science Review* 38 (1944): 540–548.

Lowi, Theodore J. "The State in Political Science: How We Become What We Study." *American Political Science Review* 86 (1992): 1–7.

———. "Public Intellectuals and the Public Interest: Toward a Politics of Political Science as a Calling." *PS: Political Science and Politics,* October (2010): 675–681.

Lukacs, Georg. *History and Class Consciousness: Studies in Marxist Dialectics,* translated by Rodney Livingstone. Cambridge, MA: The MIT Press, 1968.

Luke, Timothy W. *Screens of Power: Ideology, Domination, and Resistance in Informational Society.* Urbana: University of Illinois Press, 1989a.

———. "Political Science and the Discourses of Power: Developing a Genealogy of the Political Culture Concept." *History of Political Thought* X (1989b): 125–149.

———. *Social Theory and Modernity: Critique, Dissent, and Revolution*. London: Sage Publications, 1990.

———. "Discourses of Disintegration, Texts of Transformation: Re-reading Realism in the New World Order." *Alternatives* 18 (1993): 229–258.

———. "Toward a North American Critical Theory." *Telos* 101 (Fall, 1994): 101–180.

———. "Governmentality and Contragovernmentality: Rethinking Sovereignty and Territory after the Cold War." *Political Geography* 15 (1996): 491–507.

———. *From Nationality to Nodality: How the Politics of Being Digital Transforms Globalization*. Paper presented at the annual meeting of the American Political Science Association, September 6–8, 1998. http://ultibase.rmit.edu.au/Articles/oct98/luke2.htm. (Accessed August 20, 2008.)

———. "The Discipline as Disciplinary Normalization: Networks of Research." *New Political Science* 21 (1999): 345–363.

———. "Cyborg Enchantments: Commodity Fetishism and Human/Machine Interactions." *Strategies* 13 (2000): 39–62.

———. *Museum Politics: Power Plays at the Exhibition*. Minneapolis: University of Minnesota Press, 2002.

———. "Real Interdependence: Discursivity and Concursivity in International Politics." In *Language, Agency, and Politics in a Constructed World*, edited by Francois Debrix, 101–120. New York: M. E. Sharpe, 2003.

———. "From Pedagogy to Performativity: The Crises of Research Universities, Intellectuals and Scholarly Communication." *Telos* 131 (2005): 13–32.

———. "Unbundling the State: Iraq and the 'Recontainerization' of Rule, Production, and Identity." *Environment and Planning A* 39 (2007): 1564–1581.

Luke, Timothy W., and Patrick McGovern. "Perestroika in Political Science: Past, Present, and Future." *PS: Political Science and Politics,* October (2010): 725–727.

Lynd, Robert S. *Knowledge for What? The Place of American Social Science in American Culture*. First Printed in Princeton, NJ: Princeton University Press, 1939. Reprinted by Princeton University Press, 1967.

Lyotard, Jean-Francois. *The Postmodern Condition: A Report on Knowledge*. Translated by Geoff Bennington and Brian Massumi. Minneapolis: University of Minnesota Press, 1984.

MacIntyre, Alasdair C. *After Virtue*. Notre Dame, IN: University of Notre Dame Press, 1981.

Mandel, Ernest. *Late Capitalism,* translated by Joris de Bres. London: NLB Humanities Press, 1972.

———. *Power and Money: A Marxist Theory of Bureaucracy*. London: Verso, 1992.

Marcuse, Herbert. *One-Dimensional Man: Studies in the Ideology of Advanced Industrial Society*. Boston, MA: Beacon Press, 1964.

———. *Eros and Civilization: A Philosophical Inquiry into Freud*. Boston, MA: Beacon Press, 1966.

Marshall, T. H. *Citizenship and Social Class: And Other Essays*. Cambridge: Cambridge University Press, 1950.

———. *The Right to Welfare and Other Essays*. London: Heinmann Educational Books, 1981.

Maslow, A. H. "A Theory of Human Motivation." *Psychological Review* 50 (1943): 370–396.

McLaughlin, Neil, Lisa Kowalchuk, and Kerry Turcotte. "Why Sociology Does Not Need to Be Saved: Analytical Reflections on Public Sociologies." In *Public Sociology: The Contemporary Debate*, edited by Lawrence T. Nichols, 289–315. New Brunswick, NJ: Transaction Publishers, 2007.

McSwite, O. C. *Legitimacy in Public Administration: A Discourse Analysis.* Thousand Oaks, CA: SAGE Publications, 1997.

Merton, Robert K. *Social Theory and Social Structure.* New York: Free Press, 1957.

Miliband, Ralph. *The State in Capitalist Society.* New York: Basic Books, 1969.

Mills, C. Wright. *The Sociological Imagination.* First published in Oxford: Oxford University Press, 1959. Reprinted in New York: Oxford University Press, 2000.

Milward, H. Brinton, and Keith G. Provan. "Governing the Hollow State." *Journal of Public Administration Research and Theory* 10 (2000): 359–379.

Milward, H. Brinton, Keith G. Provan, and Barbara A. Else. "What Does the Hollow State Look Like?" In Barry Bozeman, ed. *Public Management: The State of the Art*, 309–322. San Francisco, CA: Jossey-Bass, 1993.

Mitchell, Timothy. "The Limits of the State: Beyond Statist Approaches and Their Critics." *The American Political Science Review* 85 (1991): 77–96.

———. *Rule of Experts: Egypt, Techno-Politics, Modernity.* Berkeley: University of California Press, 2002.

Mook, Lauri. "Social Accounting." In *Third Sector Research*, edited by Rupert Taylor, 171–186. New York: Springer, 2010.

Mook, Lauri, Jack Quarter, and Betty J. Richmond. *What Counts: Social Accounting for Nonprofits and Cooperatives.* Cambridge: Sigel Press, 2006.

Mouffe, Chantal. "Democracy, Power, and the 'Political'." In *Democracy and Difference: Contesting the Boundaries of the Political*, edited by Selya Benhabib, 245–256. Princeton, NJ: Princeton University Press, 1996.

———. "Deliberative Democracy or Agonistic Pluralism." *Social Research* 66 (1999): 745–758.

———. *The Return of the Political.* London: Verso, 2005.

Munck, Ronaldo. "Global Civil Society." In *Third Sector Research*, edited by Rupert Taylor, 317–326. New York: Springer, 2010.

Murphy, Alexander B. "Enhancing Geography's Role in Public Debate." *Annals of the Association of American Geographers* 96 (2006): 1–13.

Murphy, Alexander B., H. J. de Blij, B. L. Turner, Ruth Wilson Gilmore, and Derek Gregory. "The Role of Geography in Public Debate." *Progress in Human Geography* 29, no. 2 (2005): 165–193.

Murphy, Kyle Anthony. "Sociology and UNC Wilmington Goes Public." *Footnotes* 35, no. 9 (2007): 4–5.

Naidoo, Kumi, ed. *Civil Society at the Millennium.* West Hartford, CT: Kumarian Press Inc., 1999.

Najam, Adil. "NGO Accountability: A Conceptual Framework." *Development Policy Review* 14 (1996): 339–353.

National Association of Schools of Public Affairs and Administration. http://www.naspaa.org/accreditation/seeking/reference/standards.asp. (Accessed January 5, 2008.)

Neocleous, Mark. "From Civil Society to the Social." *British Journal of Sociology* 46 (1995): 395–408.

Newbold, Stephanie. "Toward a Constitutional School for American Public Administration." *Public Administration Review,* July/August (2010): 538–546.

Newman, Janet, Marian Barnes, Helen Sullivan, and Andrew Knops. "Public Participation and Collaborative Governance." *Journal of Social Policy* 33 (2004): 203–223.

Nichols, Lawrence T., ed. *Public Sociology: The Contemporary Debate.* New Brunswick, NJ: Transaction Publishers, 2007.

Nickel, Patricia Mooney. "There Is an Unknown on Campus: From Normative to Performative Violence in Academia." In *Tragedy and Terror at Virginia Tech: There Is a Gunman on Campus,* edited by Ben Agger and Timothy W. Luke, 161–186. Lanham, MD: Rowman & Littlefield, 2008.

———. "Public Intellectuality: Academies of Exhibition and the New Disciplinary Secession." *Theory and Event* 12 (2009).

Nickel, Patricia M., and Angela M. Eikenberry. "Beyond Public vs. Private: The Transformative Potential of Democratic Feminist Management." *Administrative Theory and Praxis* 28 (2006): 359–380.

———. "Responding to 'Natural' Disasters: The Ethical Implications of the Voluntary State." *Administrative Theory and Praxis* 29, no. 4 (2007): 534–545.

———. "The Discourse of Marketized Philanthropy: A Critique of Consumption, Profit, and Media Celebration as the Basis for Benevolence." *American Behavioral Scientist* 57 (2009): 974–989.

———. "Philanthropy in an Era of Global Governance." In *Third Sector Research,* edited by Rupert Taylor, 269–279. New York: Springer, 2010.

Nixon, Jon, Melanie Walker, and Stephen Baron. "From Washington Heights to the Raploch: Evidence, Mediation, and the Genealogy of Policy." *Social Policy and Society* 1, no. 3 (2002): 237–246.

Office of the Community and Voluntary Sector (OCVS). http://www.ocvs.govt.nz, 2010.

Office of the United Nations High Commissioner for Human Rights. http://www.ohchr.org/EN/Pages/WelcomePage.aspx, 2008a.

———. *Human Rights Bodies.* http://www.ohchr.org/EN/HRBodies/Pages/HumanRightsBodies.aspx, 2008b.

———. *Universal Periodic Review.* http://www.ohchr.org/EN/HRBodies/UPR/Pages/UPRMain.aspx, 2008c.

———. *Information Note for NGOs on the Human Rights Council Advisory Committee.* http://www2.ohchr.org/english/bodies/hrcouncil/advisorycommittee/ngo_participation.htm, 2008d.

Paolucci, Paul. "Public Sociology, Marxism, and Marx." In *No Social Science Without Critical Theory (Current Perspectives in Social Theory, Vol. 25),* edited by Harry Dahms, 353–382. Bingley, UK: Emerald Group Publishing Limited, 2008.

Parsons, Talcott. "Introduction." In *Knowledge and Society: American Sociology,* edited by Talcott Parsons, v–xv. Washington, DC: Voice of America Forum Lectures, 1968.

———. "'The Intellectual': A Social Role Category." In *On Intellectuals: Theoretical Studies, Case Studies,* edited by Phillip Rieff, 3–24. Garden City, NY: Doubleday & Company, 1969.

Patterson, Orlando. "About Public Sociology." In *Public Sociology: Fifteen Eminent Sociologists Debate Politics and the Profession in the Twenty-first Century*, edited by Dan Clawson, Robert Zussman, Joya Misra, Naomi Gerstel, Randall Stokes, Douglas L. Anderton, and Michael Burawoy, 176–194. Berkeley: University of California Press, 2007.

Patterson, Patricia M. "Viscera, Emotion, and Administration." *Administrative Theory and Praxis* 23 (2001): 205–230.

Perrucci, Robert, Kathleen Ferraro, JoAnn Miller, and Glenn Muschert, eds. *Agenda for Social Justice: Solutions* 2008. http://www.sssp1.org/File/Agenda_For_Social_Justice_2008.pdf. (Accessed September 2, 2010.)

Piccone, Paul. "The Crisis of One-Dimensionality." *Telos* 35 (1978): 43–54.

Pierre, Jon, ed. *Debating Governance: Authority, Steering, and Democracy*. New York: Oxford University Press, 2000.

Polanyi, Karl. *The Great Transformation*. New York: Farrar and Rinehart, 1944.

Provan, Keith G., and Patrick Kenis. "Modes of Network Governance: Structure, Management, and Effectiveness." *Journal of Public Administration Research and Theory* 18 (2008): 229–252.

Pubantz, Jerry, and John A. Moore Jr. "Promoting Peace Through Global Governance." In *Public Sociologies Reader*, edited by Judith Blau and Keri E. I. Smith, 231–248. Lanham, MD: Rowman & Littlefield Publishers, 2006.

Public Broadcasting Service. Commanding Heights: The Battle for the World Economy. "Episode 2, Chapter 9: Poland's Solidarity." DVD transcript. Heights Production, Inc., 2002a. Public Broadcasting Service, http://www.pbs.org/wgbh/commandingheights/shared/minitext/tr_show02.html#9. (Accessed August 23, 2010.)

———. Commanding Heights: The Battle for the World Economy. "Episode 1, Chapter 15: Thatcher Takes the Helm." DVD transcript. Heights Production, Inc., 2002b. Public Broadcasting Service http://www.pbs.org/wgbh/commandingheights/shared/minitext/tr_show01.html#15. (Accessed August 23, 2010.)

Purcell, Trevor W. "Public Anthropology: An Idea Searching for a Reality." *Transforming Anthropology* 9, no. 2 (2000): 30–33.

Putnam, Robert D. *Bowling Alone: The Collapse and Revival of American Community*. New York: Touchstone Books, 2000.

Putney, Norella M., Dawn E. Alley, and Vern L. Bengtson. "Social Gerontology as Public Sociology in Action." In *Public Sociology: The Contemporary Debate*, edited by Lawrence T. Nichols, 95–118. New Brunswick, NJ: Transaction Publishers, 2007.

Rhodes, R. A. W. "The New Governance: Governing Without Government." *Political Studies* 44, no. 4 (1996): 652–667.

Rodriguez, Dylan. "The Political Logic of the Non-Profit Industrial Complex." In *The Revolution Will Not Be Funded: Beyond the Non-Profit Industrial Complex*, edited by INCITE! Women of Color Against Violence, 21–41. Cambridge, MA: South End Press, 2007.

Roelofs, Joan. "Networks and Democracy: It Ain't Necessarily So." *American Behavioral Scientist* 52 (2009): 990–1005.

Rohr, John A. *To Run a Constitution; The Legitimacy of the Administrative State*. Lawrence: The University of Kansas Press, 1986.

Rothschild, Joyce. "The Collectivist Organization: An Alternative to Rational-Bureaucratic Models." *American Sociological Review* 44 (1979): 509–527.

———. "Creating a Just and Democratic Workplace: More Engagement, Less Hierarchy." *Contemporary Sociology* 29, no. 1 (2000): 195–213.

Ryan, Michael. *Marxism and Deconstruction: A Critical Articulation.* Baltimore, MD: The Johns Hopkins University Press, 1982.

Said, Edward W. *Representations of the Intellectual.* New York: Vintage Books, 1994.

Saint Louis University. *Master's Program in Public Sociology,* 2010. www.slu.edu/x15866 .xml. (Accessed December 15, 2010.)

Salamon, Lester M. "The Rise of the Nonprofit Sector." *Foreign Affairs* 73 (1994): 109–122.

———. "Putting the Civil Society Sector on the Economic Map of the World." *Annals of Public and Comparative Economics* 81 (2010): 167–210.

Salamon, Lester M., and Helmut K. Anheier. *The Emerging Nonprofit Sector: An Overview.* Manchester: Manchester University Press, 1996.

———. "Social Origins of Civil Society: Explaining the Nonprofit Sector Cross-Nationally." *Voluntas: International Journal of Voluntary and Nonprofit Organizations* 9 (1998): 213–248.

Salamon, Lester M., Helmut K. Anheier, Regina List, Stefan Toepler, S. Wojciech Sokolowski, and Associates. "Global Civil Society: Dimensions of the Nonprofit Sector." Baltimore, MD: The Johns Hopkins Center for Civil Society Studies, 1999.

Salamon, Lester M., and Odus V. Elliott. *Tools of Government: A Guide to the New Governance.* Oxford: Oxford University Press, 2002.

Salamon, Lester M., and Stephanie Lessans Geller, with the assistance of Susan C. Lorentz. "Nonprofit America: A Force for Democracy?" *The Johns Hopkins Listening Post Project, Communiqué No. 9: Nonprofit Advocacy and Lobbying.* Johns Hopkins University Center for Civil Society Studies, 2008.

Salamon, Lester M., Stephanie L. Geller, and Kasey L. Mengel. "Nonprofits, Innovation, and Performance Measurement: Separating Fact from Fiction." *Listening Post Project Communiqué No. 17: The Johns Hopkins Center for Civil Society Studies,* Baltimore, MD, 2010.

Sanders, Jackie, Mike O'Brien, Margaret Tennant, S. Wojciech Sokolowski, and Lester M. Salamon. *The New Zealand Non-profit Sector in Comparative Perspective.* Wellington: Office for the Community and Voluntary Sector, 2008.

Sassen, Saskia. "A Public Sociology for a Global Age: Recovering the Political." In *Handbook of Public Sociology,* edited by Vincent Jeffries, 391–407. Lanham, MD: Rowman and Littlefield Publishers, 2009.

Schmitter, Philippe C. "Still the Century of Corporatism?" *Review of Politics* 36 (1974): 85–131.

Schreurs, Petra. "Introduction to the 'The Ongoing Dialog on Rationality'." *Administrative Theory and Praxis* 25 (2003): 117–136.

Shils, Edward. "The Intellectuals and the Powers: Some Perspectives for Comparative Analysis." In *On Intellectuals,* edited by Philip Rieff, 25–47. Garden City, NY: Doubleday, 1969.

———. "Do We Still Need Academic Freedom?" *The American Scholar* 62, no. 2 (1993): 187–209.

Shils, Edward, and Steven Grosby, eds. *The Calling of Education: The Academic Ethic and Other Essays on Higher Education.* Chicago, IL: The University of Chicago Press, 1997.

Sirianni, Carmen. *Investing in Democracy: Engaging Citizens in Collaborative Governance.* Washington, DC: Brookings Institution Press, 2009.

Slim, Hugo. "Dissolving the Difference Between Humanitarianism and Development: The Mixing of a Rights-Based Solution." In *Development Methods and Approaches: Critical Reflections,* edited by Deborah Eade, 21–25. Oxford: Oxfam, 2003.

Smith, Andrea. "Introduction." *The Revolution Will Not Be Funded: Beyond the Non-Profit Industrial Complex,* edited by INCITE! Women of Color Against Violence, 1–18. Cambridge, MA: South End Press, 2007.

Smith, Dorothy E. *Texts, Facts, and Femininity: Exploring the Relations of Ruling.* New York: Routledge, 1990.

Sørensen, Eva. "Democratic Governance and the Changing Role of Users of Public Services." *Administrative Theory and Praxis* 22 (2000): 24–44.

———. "Democratic Theory and Network Governance." *Administrative Theory and Praxis* 24 (2002): 693–720.

———. "Democratic Problems and Potentials of Network Governance." *European Political Studies* 4 (2005): 348–357.

———. "Meta-Governance: The Changing Role of Politicians in Processes of Democratic Governance." *American Review of Public Administration* 36 (2006a): 98–114.

———. "Governance Networks and their Democratic Anchorage." *New Spaces of European Governance* (Vienna: University of Vienna Press, 2006b): 109–128.

———. "Democratic Theory as a Frame for Decision Making: The Challenges by Discourse Theory and Governance Theory." In *Handbook of Decision Making,* edited by G. Morcal, 151–168. New York: Marcel Dekker, 2007a.

———. "Local Politicians and Public Administrators as Metagovernors." In *European Studies of Democratic Network Governance,* edited by M. Marcussen and J. Torfing, 89–108. London: Palgrave Macmillan, 2007b.

Sørensen, Eva, and Jacob Torfing. "Network Politics, Political Capital and Democracy." *International Journal of Public Administration* 26 (2003): 609–634.

———. "Network Governance and Post-Liberal Democracy." *Administrative Theory and Praxis* 27 (2005a): 197–237.

———. "The Democratic Anchorage of Governance Networks." *Scandinavian Political Studies* 28 (2005b): 195–218.

———. "Theoretical Approaches to the Analysis of Governance Network Dynamics." In *Theories of Democratic Network Governance,* edited by Eva Sørensen and Jacob Torfing, 25–42. London: Palgrave, 2007a.

———. "Theoretical Approaches to Governance Network Failure and Success." In *Theories of Democratic Network Governance,* edited by Eva Sørensen and Jacob Torfing, 95–110. London: Palgrave, 2007b.

———. "Theoretical Approaches to Metagovernance." In *Theories of Democratic Network Governance,* edited by Eva Sørensen and Jacob Torfing, 169–182. London: Palgrave, 2007c.

———. "Theoretical Approaches to Democratic Network Governance." In *Theories of Democratic Network Governance,* edited by E. Sørensen and J. Torfing, 233–246. London: Palgrave, 2007d.

———. "Studying Local Network Exclusion through Observation and Diary." In *Analysing Democratic Network Governance: Methodological Issue,* edited by Peter Bogason and Metta Zølner , 148–178. London: Palgrave Macmillan, 2007e.

———. "Enhancing Effective and Democratic Governance Through Empowered Participation: Some Critical Reflections." *Planning Theory and Practice* 9 (2008): 394–399.

———. "The Politics of Self-Governance in Meso-Level Theories." In *The Politics of Self-Governance,* edited by Eva Sørensen, Jacob Torfing, and Peter Triantafillou, 43–60. London: Ashgate, 2009.

Stacey, Judith. "If I Were the Goddess of Sociological Things." In *Public Sociology: Fifteen Eminent Sociologists Debate Politics and the Profession in the Twenty-first Century,* edited by Dan Clawson, Robert Zussman, Joya Misra, Naomi Gerstel, Randall Stokes, Douglas L. Anderton, and Michael Burawoy, 91–100. Berkeley: University of California Press, 2007.

Staeheli, Lynn A. "Citizenship and the Problem of Community." *Political Geography* 27 (2008): 5–21.

Statistics New Zealand. *Counting Nonprofit Institutions in New Zealand,* www.stats.gov.nz, 2005.

Stein, Arlene. "Discipline and Publish: Public Sociology in an Age of Professionalization." In *Bureaucratic Culture and Escalating Problems: Advancing the Sociological Imagination,* edited by David Knottnerus and Bernard Phillips, 156–171. Boulder, CO: Paradigm Publishers, 2009.

Stivers, Camilla. *Bureau Men, Settlement Women: Constructing Public Administration in the Progressive Era.* Lawrence: University of Kansas Press, 2000a.

———. "Resisting the Ascendancy of Public Management: Normative Theory and Public Administration." *Administrative Theory and Praxis* 22 (March 2000b): 10–23.

Stone, Deborah A. *Policy Paradox: The Art of Political Decision Making.* New York: W. W. Norton and Company, 2002.

Taylor, Charles. "Modes of Civil Society." *Public Culture* 3 (1990): 95–118.

Taylor, Rupert. "Moving Beyond Empirical Theory." In *Third Sector Research,* edited by Rupert Taylor, 1–10. New York: Springer, 2010.

Torfing, Jacob, Eva Sørensen, and Trine Fotel. "Democratic Anchorage of Governance Networks: The Case of the Femern Belt Forum." *Planning Theory* 8 (2009): 282–308.

Tormey, Simon. "Post-Marxism, Democracy, and the Future of Radical Politics." *Democracy & Nature* 7 (2001):119–134.

Townshend, Jules. "Laclau and Mouffe's Hegemonic Project: The Story So Far." *Political Studies* 52 (2004): 269–288.

Ugalde, Antonio, and Nuria Homedes. "Latin America: Capital Accumulation, Health, and the Role of International Organizations." In *Public Sociologies Reader,* edited by Judith Blau and Keri E. I. Smith, 137–156. Lanham, MD: Rowman and Littlefield Publishers, 2006.

United Nations News Centre. "Nobel Peace Prize Laureate Wins Plaudits for Microfinance Work from Senior UN Officials." November 17, 2006. http://www.un.org/apps/news/story.asp?NewsID=20649&Cr=nobel&Cr1=prize#. (Accessed August 17, 2008.)

University of North Carolina at Wilmington Public Sociology Program. http://www .uncw.edu/soccrm/sociology.html. (Accessed December 1, 2010.)

van Gennep, Arnold. *The Rites of Passage.* Chicago: University of Chicago Press, 1909.

Van Wezemael, Joris. "The Contribution of Assemblage Theory and Minor Politics for Democratic Network Governance." *Planning Theory* 7 (2008): 165–185.

Vertovec, Steve. "Minority Associations, Networks, and Public Policies: Re-assessing Relationships." *Journal for Migration and Ethnic Studies* 25, no. 1 (1999): 21–42.

Waldo, Dwight. *The Administrative State: A Study of the Political Theory of American Public Administration.* New York: The Ronald Press Company, 1948.

Wamsley, Gary L., and James F. Wolf. *Refounding Public Administration.* Newbury Park, CA: SAGE Publications, Inc., 1990.

Ward, Lester F. *Applied Sociology.* New York: Ginn & Company, 1906.

Warren, Mark E. *Democracy and Association.* Princeton, NJ: Princeton University Press, 2000.

Weber, Max. "Bureaucracy." In *Classical Sociological Theory,* edited by Craig Calhoun, Joseph Gerteis, James Moody, Steven Pfaff, and Indermohan Virk, 264–273. Oxford: Blackwell Publishing, 2007.

White, Geoffrey M. "Introduction: Public History and National Narrative." *Museum Anthropology* 21, no. 1 (1997): 3–7.

White, Orion F. Jr. "The Ideology of Technocratic Empiricism and the Discourse Movement in Contemporary Public Administration: A Clarification." *Administration and Society* 30 (1998): 471–476.

Yanow, Dvora. "American Ethnogenesis and Public Administration." *Administration and Society* 27 (1996): 483–509.

———. "Translating Local Knowledge at Organizational Peripheries." *British Journal of Management* 15 (2004): S9–S25.

Yergin, Daniel, and Joseph Stanislaw. *Commanding Heights: The Battle for the World Economy.* New York: Simon & Schuster, 2002.

Zadek, Simon. "Global Collaborative Governance: There Is No Alternative." *Corporate Governance* 8 (2008): 374–388.

Index

Credits

Parts of Chapters One and Two were first published in *Sociology Compass* 4:9, 2010 and are reprinted here with the permission of John Wiley & Sons. Copyright © 2010 Patricia Mooney Nickel and John Wiley & Sons. Some of the framing ideas in Chapter One were first published in *Theory and Event* 12:4, 2009. Reprinted with permission by The Johns Hopkins University Press. Copyright © 2009 Patricia Mooney Nickel and The Johns Hopkins University Press. Parts of Chapters Two and Three were first published in *Administration and Society* 41:2, 2009. SAGE Journals Online: http://online .sagepub.com. Reprinted with the permission of SAGE Publications. All rights reserved © 2009 Patricia Mooney Nickel and SAGE Publications Ltd./SAGE Publications, Inc. Parts of Chapters Two and Three were first published in *Current Perspectives on Social Theory* 26, 2009. Reprinted here with permission of Emerald Group Publishing. Copyright © 2009 Patricia Mooney Nickel and Emerald Group Publishing. Parts of Chapter Five were first published in *Administrative Theory and Praxis* 29:2, 2007. Reprinted here with permission of M. E. Sharpe, Inc. Copyright © 2009 Patricia Mooney Nickel and M. E. Sharpe, Inc. Parts of Chapters Five and Six were first published in *Journal of Power* 2:3, 2009. Reprinted here with permission of Taylor & Francis Group. http://www.informaworld.com. Copyright © 2009 Patricia Mooney Nickel and Taylor & Francis Group. Parts of Chapter Seven were first published in *Current Sociology* 58:3, 2010. SAGE Journals Online: http://online.sagepub. com. Reprinted with permission of SAGE Publications. All rights reserved © 2010 Patricia Mooney Nickel and SAGE Publications Ltd./SAGE Publications, Inc.

About the Author

Patricia Mooney Nickel is a political sociologist and critical social theorist in the School of Social and Cultural Studies at Victoria University of Wellington. She has published in the areas of critical social theory, public sociology, philanthropy and the nonprofit sector, and the sociology of governing. She is currently beginning work on a project that explores the themes of North American critical theory after postmodernism.